A Countryman's Glimpse of the Twentieth Century

by David Balkwill

Published by:

The Aveton Gifford Parish Project Group

Editor: Delia Elliott

Design: Neil Cooper

Printed and bound by: Nick Walker Printing Ltd
Kingsbridge, Devon. TQ7 1EQ

I dedicate this book to Sheila.

Not only was she a wonderful wife and mother but she found time to help with the school, the Sunday School and was a leading performer in the W.I. Drama Group and she also visited the sick and lonely in the village. In later years she cared for my parents with love and devotion.

CONTENTS

Preface

This memoir was written at the turn of the century at the time when material was being gathered for the book `Aveton Gifford a Heritage` published in 2002 by The Parish Project Group. Parts of the memoir form a chapter in that book. The manuscript was revisited, and the decision was made to publish this unique record of village life and farming in the 20th century.

The memoir gives a unique account of a life in farming by a man who was, and still is passionate about rural life. The unique nature of the South Hams landscape dictated the farming methods that were developed. David and his father Henry Balkwill chose to farm, there is a passion for farming and the countryside which shines through the narrative. David was very fortunate in being tutored in traditional farming methods at a time when the horse was giving way to the tractor. As a young man he experienced the effect of the depression in farming in the 1930's, and then the onset of the war which was to have such a devastating effect on the whole parish and his family in particular. On a positive note the war was to bring him love in the form of Sheila Moore who came to the farm as a Land Girl, there followed a long and very happy marriage. Sadly Sheila passed away in 2002. David lives quietly in the village continuing a keen interest in current affairs and countryside matters. He loves his garden where he grows flowers and vegetables. His constant companion and guard is his faithful Jack Russell terrier `Trix`.

His gift for descriptive writing continues to find a voice through regular articles in the church and parish magazines.

CHAPTER ONE

My Father

As we reach the beginning of the year two thousand and I enter the evening of my life, it has been suggested that I write down my interpretation of the changes which have occurred in rural life during the nineteen hundreds. As I was born a quarter of the way through this period, I have to rely on tales which have been related to me by my father, mother, and others about farming life before I was born. The narration is more of an autobiography than I would have liked, but what happened to us is reflected in the lives of everyone connected to agriculture in the South Hams.

Balkwill Family History

I come from a family traced historically by a cousin with more courage than I would have had, for fear of digging up a collection of rogues. His search culminated with a Norman named De Bacqeville at the time of the Conquest who settled at Peters Marland in North Devon. A branch later moved to Bere Alston. Then in 1750 another off-shoot moved to Yarde Farm, Malborough. They had eight children, and one son Richard married a girl called Elizabeth Hancock from Stoke Damerel on the Tamar in 1804, and farmed at Ilton Castle near Salcombe. I suppose she kept returning home to mother, and bearing in mind the length and perilous nature of the journey on horseback, (her mother-in-law Hannah had already seen off a highwayman at the top of Aveton Gifford Hill) was absent from home for long periods. Richard wrote many letters to her when she was away which survived, thus providing those of us who came after an insight into the difficult farming conditions which existed at the time, the production and sale of malt (fermented barley) and cider, plus the continual conflict with the excise men. He and his brother who farmed at Burton Farm, Galmpton purchased a boat to take their produce out of the district, and there is little doubt they brought illicit goods back in. This business thrived, culminating in a beautiful, fast, new ship named 'The Briza' which was built in Liverpool, much to the annoyance of the boat builders on the Salcombe Estuary who had previously done their work.

Balkwill Family Tree

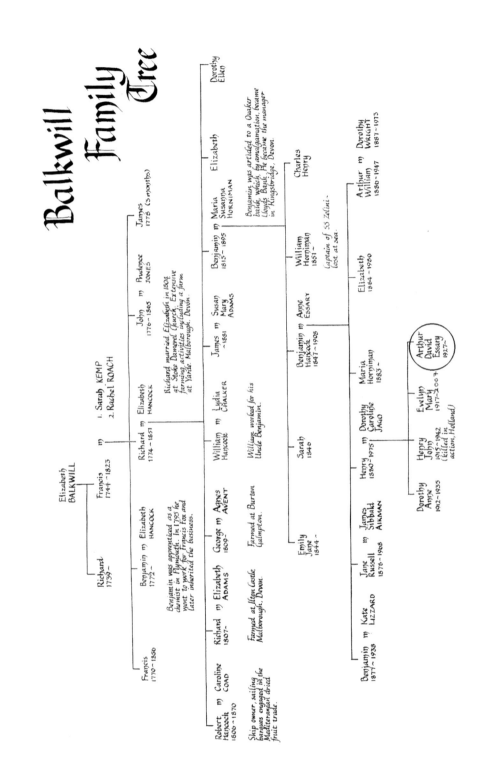

Elizabeth BALKWILL

Richard 1759~   Francis 1744~1823 m 1. Sarah KEMP 2. Rachel ROACH

Benjamin 1772~ m Elizabeth HANCOCK
Benjamin was apprenticed as a chemist in Plymouth. In 1795 he went to work for Francis Fox and later inherited the business.

Richard 1774~1851 m Elizabeth HANCOCK
Richard married Elizabeth in 1804 at Stoke Damerel Church. Extensive farming activities including a farm at Yarde Malborough. Devon.

John 1776~1865 m Prudence JONES

James 1776 (3 months)

Francis 1770~1850

Robert Hancock 1800~1870 m Caroline COAD
Ship owner, sailing barques engaged in the Mediterranean dried fruit trade.

Richard 1807~ m Elizabeth ADAMS
Farmed at Ilton Castle, Malborough. Devon.

George 1809~ m Agnes AVENT
Farmed at Burton Galmpton.

William Hancock m Lydia CHALKER
William worked for his Uncle Benjamin.

James ~1881 m Susan Mary ADAMS

Benjamin 1815~1895 m Maria Susanna HORNIMAN
Benjamin was articled to a Quaker bank, which, by amalgamation, became Lloyds Bank. He became the manager in Kingsbridge, Devon.

Elizabeth

Dorothy Ellen

Emily Jane 1844~

Sarah 1840

Benjamin Hancock 1847~1908 m Anne ESSARY

William Horniman 1851~ (Captain of SS Zelini~ lost at sea.)

Charles Henry

Benjamin 1877~1938 m Kate LIZZARD

Jane Russell 1876~1968 m James Sibbald AIKMAN

Henry 1880~1975 m Dorothy Caroline JAGO

Maria Horniman 1883~

Elizabeth 1864~1950

Arthur William 1880~1947 m Dorothy WRIGHT 1887~1975

Dorothy Anne 1912~1935

Henry John 1915~1942 (killed in action, Holland)

Evelyn Mary 1917~2007

Arthur David Essary 1927~

This boat was specifically built for the fruit trade from the Canary Islands, a many-masted, slender, piece of excellence, which when in full sail must have taken the breath away from those watching. I saw a painting of her when new, and another five years later, by which time her masts were bent into a curve with the force of the wind. She was eventually lost off an island in the West Indies. It has been said my forebears lost out in the shipping business by their reluctance to turn over to steam.

My father was born on 15th September 1880 at Launceston and moved to Kingsbridge at the age of four when my grandfather was appointed manager of the branch of the then Devon and Cornwall Bank, subsequently to be taken over by Lloyds Bank. He succeeded my great grandfather. In those days it was quite accepted that a son could follow his father into the bank hierarchy.

My father had a Methodist upbringing and was taught at Sunday school by his father who was not averse to flicking the ears of misbehaving boys with his forefinger in such a way that it was not soon forgotten. From primary school he went on to the Kingsbridge Grammar School where the headmaster was a sadistic beater of boys. Holidays were spent on an uncle's farm near Launceston, and on leaving school my father wanted to take a career in farming. His father had other ideas, fuelled no doubt by looking at farming accounts during the agricultural recession at the end of the last century, and sent him into the clothing trade in London.

A Cotswold Farm

How long he stuck that I do not recall, but he hated it and took on a partner to rent a small farm in the Cotswolds near Cheltenham. His partner developed a liking for hunting, and according to my father some of the riders rode side saddle. The partnership did not last long and they parted company. I don't know whether it was that which created his dislike for the hunting fraternity, the experience of forty riders ploughing through his sodden field of wheat, or being ignored by the same riders in Cheltenham High Street. When I was growing up he would always co-operate with the huntsman, whom he respected, but treated the hierarchy and followers with disdain. Cheltenham High Street was a snooty place he told me, deliveries to shops from farms had to be very early, horse drawn deliveries were banned in that street after eight a.m.

The farm was heavy clay, ploughed in ten foot wide strips. About a dozen furrows ploughed one way and a dozen furrows ploughed back against them, leaving an open furrow between the strips for drainage. Four horses were needed in line ahead of a single furrow plough to turn the sticky soil, with a boy beside the horses making sure there were no slackers. This was an ideal situation to train a young horse, which would be placed either second or third in line. 'Breaking in a colt' was the terminology.

Dad told me of an incident on a neighbour's farm. A horseman was breaking in a young horse in similar fashion. The colt was temperamental, the horseman was content to let him walk along without pulling, knowing that in time he would settle down and learn to pull his share. The boss arrived to inspect the ploughing, and noticing the shirking youngster, castigated his employee for allowing the colt to idle, then rode up beside the offender and slashed him with his whip. The colt went berserk, rearing up and turning around several times, getting so tangled up in the chains and injuring himself so badly that eventually he had to be put down. This was Dad's way of advising me that gentleness with livestock invariably brought the best results.

Ploughing was very heavy work for the horses. If it was wet they sometimes would stop on their own accord halfway through a field shaking with the effort and blowing with nostrils wide open until after a rest they were able to continue. Also hairy-legged horses such as shires would collect glutinous mud around their fetlocks and were scarcely able to put one leg in front of the other until the ploughman scraped the mud away. A half to three quarters of an acre a day was the normal target.

The Gypsy Camp

Their farm was close to a gypsy camp which must have been stationary (on a permanent site) according to the tales I was told. One man was called Rhymes, an expert hedger for the thorn hedges of that district. Whenever in later years I attempted to repair the totally different hedges of Court Barton I was quoted Rhymes chapter and verse. The gypsies had a good eye for horses. When Father wanted a horse he would let it be known to Rhymes and in due course a horse would arrive for inspection. On one occasion the horse brought to him showed too much white of eye and had four white socks on its legs. Dad recalled the rhyme about horse buying.

One white stocking buy him, two white stockings try him,

Three white stockings doubt him, four white stockings do without him.

Forever fearful of a gypsy curse, he carefully and politely declined to buy.

"That's alright Master" said the Gypsy, *"I'll take him around the reverse way".*

Later asking Rhymes what the horse dealer meant, he learnt that the horse had been hawked around the whole of the county of Gloucester one way and now would be taken back around the other way.

On the whole Dad described them as a very gentle people and fine workers. He had no hang-ups (reservations) when they came looking for scrap iron or hawking their handicrafts when I was a youngster. Mother often bought wooden clothes pegs made from hedgerow spindle. Most of our neighbours never had a good word to say about them and would order them off the premises. Gypsy family disputes that Dad described would bring out a primitive savagery in them which had to be seen to be believed. Always one to one, the men would back off thirty to forty yards before rushing at one another like a couple of rams in combat, whilst the other members of the clan observed patiently until one of the contestants capitulated before they administered first aid. Female disputes were settled hand to hand with biting, a lot of kicking, scratching, and tearing of hair.

Court Barton

Mum and Dad married in 1911 and when war broke out in 1914 Dad volunteered to join the army and was turned down because he had flat feet. This was a disappointment, but determined to do something to help the war effort he volunteered for ambulance duty, thus catching a dose of fleas from wounded soldiers returning from the trenches on the Somme. The dislike of fleas and fear of fire, particularly in thatch, remained with him all his life. I could never understand the logic of those neuroses as fleas mostly lived in thatch.

Court Barton late 19th century

In 1919, together with three children, an Old English sheepdog, and a Welsh cob, they came to Court Barton, Aveton Gifford, a holding then of nearly two hundred acres. The farm had been rented by three brothers; with a sister keeping house they were most resentful that the farm had been sold without their knowledge so they offered no help to the incoming occupiers. For years they had lambed the ewes in the courtyard by the backdoor. Dad was warned by the local vet to change this practice or suffer the consequence of joint ill in the lambs.

The other immediate requirement was horses, a scarce commodity in the aftermath of war. Dad acquired the help of a 'horsey' neighbour to help him choose the best, and described to me a sale he attended at Bigbury Court with his horse buyer. The two horses the man bought fetched the top prices and were given a round of applause by the assembled company. When he told me the story Dad ruefully commented:

"He got the applause, but it was my money."

Court Barton with family terrier Gyp. 1932

The farm buildings at Court had been burnt down in the 1850's and been rebuilt with the horse firmly in mind as the means of power. Apparently the then owner had used direct labour in the rebuilding and used old ship's timbers for the doorways and windows, much to the disgust of the village master builders.

Farming in this hilly district was very alien to coping with flat land made up of heavy clay and Dad had to rely on the farm workers to initiate him into local farming practices, sowing times and harvesting techniques. The farmworkers were three horsemen and an odd job man who could drive a team of horses when needed, a stockman who looked after the sheep, the young cattle and would help milk if needed, a dairymaid and a housemaid. Dad would also employ a lad of fourteen for a year or until the youngster was able to get an apprenticeship to one of the various tradesmen in the village. There were carpenters, joiners, masons, butchers, farriers etc.

My sister Molly (Evelyn Mary) on our Welsh cob Court Barton c. 1930

There were no tied cottages attached to the farm, all the men lived in the village. Being used to the flat terrain of the previous farm, the dog was alright about the yard but refused to gather the sheep off the hilly pastures. The stout-hearted little cob fared better though even he found Kingsbridge Hill an awesome prospect. In those days it wasn't a more or less even slope it is today, but three steep inclines, one at the bottom, one beside Creacombe, and one at the top. It was he that pulled the trap with produce to market or the family on a shopping expedition in Kingsbridge. There was no fear of the dog repeating what had happened on a trip into Cheltenham. He had followed Dad on that occasion unseen by walking under the trap close to the cob's heels, but was spotted by a policeman. The result was an appearance before the magistrates and a fine of four shillings and sixpence for having a dog on the highway without a collar.

I think this must have made Dad wary of policemen. The village constabulary was opposite what is now the village hall, complete with tiny cell for locking up drunks until they sobered up. The garden backed on to Pulleys Meadow and when the resident bobby asked Dad if he could cut a hole in the fence to let his hens have run of the meadow, he very quickly acquiesced.

"I would have let him have two if he had asked, one hole for the hens to come out and one for going back in, because that policeman was hot."

The whole of farming life was dictated by the speed of the horse. The only mechanised contraption was the steam engine which toured the farms to thresh out the ricks of corn during the winter. Almost all the grain was home fed, a little barley was sold for malting in a good year. There was a small threshing machine in one of the barns, (I suspect even then it was being superseded by the travelling thresher), a crusher to make the grain more palatable for horses was installed close to the thresher, the whole driven by up to four horses on a carousel from the roundhouse next door by an ingenious system of cogs, pulleys and belts. (*David can remember as a small boy sitting on the back of one of the horses walking around in the roundhouse.*)

Livestock was driven to market either in Kingsbridge or Modbury. Small livestock would be taken by trap or cart and dressed poultry at Christmas in a wagon. My mother sold butter, eggs and milk at the door. There was no refrigeration. Pans of milk had to be carried a good two hundred yards across the orchard to the butter well, a small cavern built over a spring bubbling up through a seam in the rock. It was the coolest water on the farm. Not far from there was another spring emptying into a pond close to the track which led to the rest of the fields on that side of the road. The horses always paused there to drink on coming back from working in the fields.

Kingsbridge Market 1930.

The Cider Ration

It was the custom to give a quart of cider to each workman daily as part of his wages. It was the boy's job to get the key to the cellar from the house, measure out the cider into each man's quart stone jar, then return the key to the house.

It was past six o'clock one evening when Dad returned from market to see four horses out in the orchard still harnessed for ploughing, grazing between the apple trees. Every time they put their heads down to graze, their collars would slip from their shoulders to the back of their heads, they would eat a few mouthfuls then throw the collars back against their shoulders with a toss of their heads. Dad was mystified and inwardly angry that the men had not seen to their horses properly. As he neared the gate he heard moaning coming from the pond and found the two horsemen spread-eagled in the mud beside the pond. Somehow they had managed to get hold of the key to the cellar and had taken gallons of cider to the field instead of pints. Men always rode bareback and sideways on the horse to the field they were working in, and back to the stable. They managed to mount their horses by climbing on the ploughs but tumbled off when the horses put their heads down to drink at the pond. Dad's anger turned to alarm. What if the horses had waded farther and deeper into the pond? Would the men have sobered up or drowned?

Steam driven corn thresher - cider jars evident!

Anyway he decided to stop the men's daily cider ration, close down the cider press and the pound, and pay the men extra in lieu of the cider. This caused ructions and some men left, but he had made up his mind. What happened to the culprits? I do not know, but I always wondered what the ploughing was like. From then on the orchard went into decline.

A Terrible Accident

It was about this time my sister then aged five had a terrible accident. She wore her hair in long tresses and got too close to the belts driving the crusher in the barn. Her hair became entangled and her scalp was nearly torn from her head. The horses in the roundhouse next door driving the machinery felt the extra strain and stopped. The lad who was attending the horses went into the barn, saw the little girl trapped in the machinery and called to another man for help. Together they cut off the hair which was trapped, and had the presence of mind to replace the torn scalp. There was a doctor in the house attending to my father who had shingles: whether he stitched the scalp back on or applied first aid is still open to family argument. She was taken to hospital in Plymouth by horse ambulance, eventually making a full recovery with no long term discomfort. It was an accident which shocked the farming community. For fifty years people from all around the district would approach me and ask after my sister. Sadly no one asks me these days because all those who remembered have passed on.

The family were lucky in having a doctor in the house at the time of the accident. A farm worker told me several years later that he had run the four miles into Modbury to fetch a doctor for his sick wife and was not offered a lift back in the trap but he was allowed to hold on to the back to help him along. He said if it was raining you might get offered a lift, but if you caught the pony from the field, harnessed it and put it between the shafts then you could be pretty sure of the ride. On reflection, one of the advantages horses have over their tractor successors is that should they feel a sudden extra pull they will stop, thus avoiding damaging machinery or in my sister's case further terrible injury. With tractors the only indication is the opening of the governors in the engine and by the time the clutch is depressed the machine being pulled is bent, if not twisted beyond recognition.

Old Harry

I never quite figured out the role of 'Old Harry', a loyal employee and confidante. Dad always called him 'my foreman'. Mangels, or mangolds as they were called locally were the staple diet of the cattle in winter. Dad was never over enthusiastic because they were not grown on the heavy clay of Gloucestershire and therefore he had no experience, whereas mangolds and swedes collectively called 'roots' thrive in the damp West Country. Old Harry would go on about the feed value of mangolds and Dad would say:

"Hang on a minute! Mangolds are more than eighty per cent water."

A puzzled Harry would reply, *"I don't believe'ee Maister, but if you be right there must be a 'elluva lot of whisky in the water."*

There must have been an incentive to grow sugar beet at one time, because it was decided to grow a crop. I never asked him if he had grown them before, but he must have gone into their viability. The finished beet were to be transported to Loddiswell railway station en route to the factory by horse and cart along the road by Knap Mill, Millers Path via the road by Rake Quarry. He grew them in the field closest to Knap Mill. He even had extra boards fitted to the carts to carry heavier loads because it was almost level pulling all the way. Alas the sugar beet grew two roots like giant molars and the only gas to extract them out of the ground was the bad language of the chap who had to pull them. They were never grown again. They seemed to take much notice of rhymed adages. My mother's favourite was always:

"Lock up in your barn until Candlemas[1] day, Two thirds of your corn and half your hay."

This was to ensure there would be enough sustenance to feed the horses through the spring work, but it was always in my mother's nature to hoard. All the crops grown at that time were sown in the spring, the exception in East Anglia would be winter wheat. Here in the South Hams the winters were too mild; it was not until the 1950's with the advent of effective fungicides to control leaf borne diseases that the switch was made to autumn sown crops.

---

[1] 4 February, the feast of the Purification of the Virgin Mary, when candles are blessed.

Early Memories

I was born in 1927, almost ten years after the sister next to me. My mother called me an afterthought, my father said I was a mistake. I had a nursemaid, a tall long legged girl who lived just above the King's Arms, which after three name changes in my lifetime is now the Fisherman's Rest.

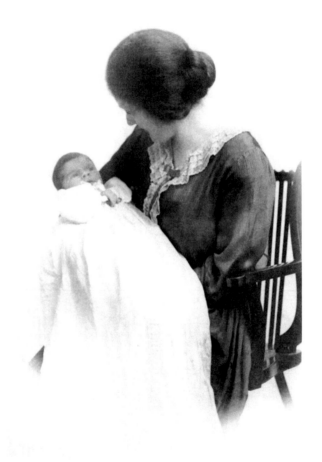

David in christening gown with mother

She used to run down the hill past Tree Farm and was halfway along the village before she slowed to a walk pushing the pram. The whirring of the wheels was my earliest memory. I was never out of the conveyance in the village simply because I would be too slow for my nanny, which prompted a question to me according to my mother from a woman with six children, who in turn was one of fourteen:

"Can't ee' walk or won't they let 'ee?"

The road must have been well maintained: it was in the early twenties when tar was first used. Before the use of tar to bind the road's surface big potholes kept appearing. Women would collect the big carboniferous stones, locally called wittaker stones, off the fields for two shillings (10p) a ton. These would be dumped in heaps at the side of the road for someone, usually from the workhouse, to break and fill the potholes. I can understand why farmers wanted them picked up. When I was learning to plough with horses the ploughshare got caught up in one of these stones, making the plough handles swing into my ribs causing very severe bruising. When tarring the roads was first introduced the tar was heated in a big iron pot pulled by horses, poured over the road, then swept over the whole of the surface with special brooms, followed by expertly scattered chippings over the tar. I have seen roadmen burning iron rakes in latter years, but how does one get tar off brooms and horses feet?

David showing early interest in livestock c.1931 *(note gin-trap on fence post)*

Studio portrait 1932

I was adored by all the female work force and must have been spoilt. I was allowed to help Old Harry with his beloved mangolds. The root house was one storey below the level of the yard with a hole in the wall at ground level, complete with a swinging board to keep the rain out. The carts at lifting time turned at this hole, backed on to it and were tipped, thus disgorging the loads into the root house. Some of the mangolds would be a lot bigger than a man's head and would helter-skelter down the growing heap with great velocity. Harry's job was to throw the roots away from the tiphole until eventually they were piled to the roof. The exit to the cows' house was boarded up with small planks which would be removed when the time came to feed them. I would help Harry by throwing back the smallest roots. When the cart came with the next load Harry would grab me, carrying me as far away from the tumbling roots as possible.

In winter Harry would feed the cows along the walkway in front of their cribs with a maundful each. A maund was a wicker basket made by the Woodmason family from the osier beds at Duke's Mill.

Mr. Woodmason with basket at Duke's Mill

I loved this job, I can hear them crunching the roots and smell their hot breaths to this day. The cows loved them too and would not take long to eat a basketful. Very occasionally a piece would get stuck in a cow's gullet; Harry would grab the cow by its nose and push his hand down the cow's throat to remove the offending piece. I have done this since when we fed the cows potatoes: it takes a great deal of strength and skill to avoid the hand being crushed by the cow's back teeth. They also had a full pitchfork or prangful of hay between two cows.

Swifts

Harry had a great fund of country knowledge. I must have asked him as many questions as my young grandson asks his father today. I can see him now on a wagon in early July forking the last of the hay into the barn above the cowshed. Perhaps it was his seniority which enabled him to choose his jobs, preferring to be outside the barn rather than in the dust and heat inside where two fellow workers forked the hay away from the doorway bathed in sweat.

Swifts were screaming around the yard.

"What are they Mr Harry?"

Harry would pause, lean on his prang and follow the swifts around with his eyes.

"They be swifts Young Maister!"

"What are they screaming for?"

"There's two old birds and four young uns. Mother and Father be teaching they to fly. I reckons they scream just for the 'ell of it. Tis one of the wunnerful zounds of zummer an' they'll be gone in a month's time."

"Where do they go Mr Harry?"

"Africa zo they zay."

I was told I must show respect by calling him mister. He in turn called me young master or 'me buck', a term I have not heard for thirty years.

David on his first pony 'Beauty' in his Twyford School uniform
outside Little Court 1933

With Prince 1936

Feeding his pets outside back door of Little Court 1936

The speed with which I picked up the dialect must have exasperated my mother who was educated at Cheltenham Ladies' College. I remember being urged to speak properly as well being told how to hold my knife and fork correctly before visiting her parents in Plymouth.

Dressed up as a knight outside Court Barton

(Chainmail made by mother from dishcloths. Church Fete 1936)

Haymaking

As well as the loft over the cows, there was a loft over the horses, which caused friction between horseman and cowman on who should have the best hay. When the lofts were full the rest of the hay was ricked out in the field where it was grown. On reflection I suppose they would have brought a couple of wagon loads in at night to give the chaps work to do in the morning while waiting for the dew to burn off. If there was one rick left at the end of the winter it would usually be the best. If it was a hungry time, the cowman would want it for his cows, the horseman for his horses, the shepherd for his sheep and Dad would probably want it for next year.

Haymaking was a labour consuming job. A wooden pole made up of two sections was erected some forty foot high with a swinging gantry like the yard arm of a sailing ship; this had a pulley on the end through which a stout wire cable ran. A horse was attached to one end of the cable and a grab made up of four iron prongs was fixed to the other end. The hay would have been windrowed (raked into rows, allowing it to dry). A horse pulling a sweep would walk up the line of hay until the sweep was full, then pulled out of the line and driven to the foot of the pole. The sweep would be tipped over the load of hay by pulling the sweep back a little, then lifted by the handles so that the toes would stick in the ground. The horse would be told to walk on, the sweep would then somersault over the load of hay, then be taken back to the field without stopping to continue up the line of hay and filled once more.

The grab would be fixed into the hay left by the sweep and the prongs locked. The pole horse would pull the hay up to a height above the rick and the man on the ground would hand over the guide rope to the men on the rick. Then they would pull the grab load of hay to the position required and trip the lock so that the hay spilled out on to the rick. Finally the guide rope was thrown back to the man on the ground and the horse backed to allow the grab to return to earth.

I have explained the operation in detail to inform the reader of the number of men required. Two on the rick, two on the ground, two if not three sweeps if it was a large field, plus a man scraping down the loose hay from the sides of the rick so that the rick builder could see they were straight, not an easy task on sloping ground. It was a source of great indignity and ribald comment if the builder had to put a prop into a bulging side. The rick was made so that a twenty rung ladder could reach the eaves for thatching. An ash ladder was very heavy, it was considered that a ladder of twenty rungs or staves could be lifted upright by one man. The thatcher would have a smaller ladder attached to the long ladder to reach the ridge.

Building a haystack using a 'hay pole'

Hay sweep in action

Thatched cornricks

In later years father had a petrol driven elevator which saved a man and a horse. One engine we had was sometimes very difficult to start; he did not understand machinery and would tear his hair out watching a gang of haymakers, each thinking they knew all about engines trying to start it up, especially if it looked like rain. Then he would long for the days of the haypole, but even they could be dangerous. If the pole snapped and fell across the rick it could badly injure a man, or if a careless sweep driver hit the stay wires holding up the pole it would come crashing to the ground. He bought a tractor once when he had a farm pupil who thought he understood machinery. He did not keep it long because it was out of action more than it was going. Apparently the pupil would drive it under a tree, then take all day to take it to pieces and put it back together again. It must have been a Fordson Standard which first appeared during the Great War. It was not updated until 1944 and then had only two forward and one reverse gear. Compare that with the American tractors imported during the Second World War, some of which had six forward gears.

Milking

Co-ordinated milk collection was beginning. At first the pick up point was California Cross at six o'clock in the morning, then it was Loddiswell Butts. Hines of Loddiswell had started a haulage business and had the contract. Dad would take two churns in the back of the trap, one for the evening's milk and one for the morning's. In the height of summer it would only be the morning milk, as the evening milk would have gone off before it reached the factory at Totnes. I went with him occasionally. I remember it being so cold that I lay on the floor behind the front board with a rug over me; it was made of sheep's wool on one side and leather on the other and it was very snug. We were usually behind time and never stopped on the journey, but one morning Dad pulled into a wide place, went to the head of the cob and told me to listen. I could hear shouting and galloping hooves. Soon three riders came bursting into view going hell for leather, arms and legs beating their mount's sides. They never hesitated when they saw us, a greeting to father came wafting back over their slipstream. According to Dad this was a once a year occurrence. Three local farmers would spend the day rabbiting at Stockadon, no doubt accompanied by a barrel of cider, have a huge supper, then play `Nap` (Napoleon - a five card game played for money) all night. Just on daybreak they would saddle their horses and race each other back to the finishing line. Guess where? The Commercial Inn.

I learnt to milk when I was five, on an old, easy cow to milk. I think she was a Guernsey called Daisy. Directly behind the cows was a dung channel, cleaned out once a day after the morning milking when the cows were turned out into fields to graze, or in winter for exercise. Perhaps I got tired of milking Daisy and wanted to try another cow, I cannot recall. But I do remember a cow kicking me into the slimy dung channel with the bucket of milk neatly covering my head. That put me off milking cows for a couple of years.

The Bull

It was just before this that the bull Dad kept went mad. I suppose he was pastured in Pulleys Meadow during the summer and any cow which came into season was turned in with him. It was said the school children had upset the bull by teasing him over the school wall. Anyway one evening he turned really nasty, pacing up and down inside the fence opposite the house, roaring and rattling the gate with his horns and charging anyone who went near. The stockman had gone home and although his dog was chained up in the stable, it would not work for Dad. So the stockman had to be fetched.

He was a man of stubborn independence. Dad used to grow roots to sell to the moorland farmers for eating off in the early months of the year. The roots would be parted off in acre sized paddocks with wire netting, and when one paddock was bare they were given another. The sheep were wild and difficult to restrain; it was the stockman's routine to take them a bag of crushed oats first thing in the morning to keep them settled. If Dad wanted him to do anything else urgently, it was always:

"I've got to see they sodding sheep fust or else they'll be gone."

He was an early riser and would come to work at 4 a.m. if needed but resented being called back to the farm after he had gone home. He strongly objected to women gossiping on the doorstep and expected his long suffering wife to come in and shut the door when he arrived in from work. My mother painted the scene for me later.

By the time the stockman got to the farm a crowd of onlookers had gathered, clinging to the roof of the church porch, peering through the gate panels, crowding along the top of the church wall and hiding behind anything they thought protected them. The stockman had fetched his dog and was about to open the gate when he saw his spectators. Leaning on his stick he addressed them as being yellow-livered and born out of wedlock. Then opening the gate he sent the dog in to bring on the bull, cursed the bull colourfully and gave him an almighty whack with his stick. The bull never looked at him, just walked meekly into the yard to his pen.

The bull was eventually shot by the vet and cut up by the local butcher. I must have badgered my nanny to take me to see it, because I distinctly remember the head lying severed from the rest of the carcass which was being cut up. Its eyes were wide open staring at me through the doorway with me hiding behind my nanny's skirt. The vet (Billy Steer) was a crack shot. When my mother wanted the guinea fowl, or gleanies as we called them, reduced in numbers, he would come up at roosting time and shoot them off the rafters of the big barn with a .22 rifle and always neatly through the head, despite the gloom.

Little Court

Times were bad financially and Dad had to shed some labour. He also began to get heart trouble, "tired heart" the doctor called it, little wonder as he was getting up at three in the morning to milk the cows and having to be at California Cross by six. The lorry would not wait if anyone was late. He was so keen that I should farm that they rented off two thirds of the land, keeping the Little Court side, building a bungalow on it and keeping half of the buildings. These were tough times yet they commissioned two poultry houses to be built by Mr Luckraft, a village carpenter, to hold five hundred hens each. They retained one man. I expect old Harry retired. I know Dad gave him three hundredweight[2] of coal each Christmas until he died.

By then cheap imports of grain, particularly maize, were flooding in from North America, so our portion of the farm was laid down to grass and only two horses were kept. We had about twelve cows, the normal number one man was expected to milk. Dad would help out mornings and I would milk a few cows afternoons after school and at weekends. Anyone who has never milked twelve cows by hand cannot understand the sheer slog it was. In our case the dairy was on the north end of the building for coolness and the cow stalls faced east. The sun poured into the doors and windows on summer afternoons behind the cows and sweat would pour off the milker into the bucket held between his

---

[2] Approximately 150kg

knees. Yet conversely it was good to feel the warmth of the cows on frosty mornings in winter.

By the time I was ten in 1938 things were looking up financially. Dad reckoned the formation of the Milk Marketing Board heralded the turn around, quite apart from the antics of the Nazis in Germany. Dad decided to join the accredited scheme for milk production and the premium bull scheme. The cowman had to attend classes for clean milk production and passed the test. The cows had to be dry milked, no spitting on your hands to make them moist or squirting milk over them either. My hands used to get so hot I kept a bucket of clean water to plunge them in between cows. The water had to be piped to the dairy and analysed as fit for milk production, each cow's flanks had to be brushed and her teats washed and dried before milking. The stools and buckets had to be kept scrupulously clean.

The Premium Bull Scheme

The premium bull scheme involved proven sires. That is bulls whose daughters had been recorded to give more milk over several lactations than their mothers. The premium bull for this parish was kept at Titwell, a mile and a half away. Only the best milkers were taken there because of the distance. It would take the whole of the morning after milking to take the cow there with three persons to cover the side lanes and open gateways. Sometimes having got there the cow would refuse to oblige, which meant waiting another three weeks before she was ready again. We only wanted daughters for breeding and invariably got bull calves; imagine the joy when we got a nice heifer calf. For the other cows we used a neighbour's bull.

I think Dad always paid his workers at the end of the week; he certainly did when I started to take an interest in the farm. In some parts of the country workers were hired for twelve months from Martinmas. (11th November Saint Martin's Day - historically hiring fairs were held where farm labourers would seek new posts). After being paid, they took a week off to buy clothing and to look for work on another farm at the various hiring fairs. They would not be paid again until the end of the following year. They could only afford one pair of corduroy trousers, one pair of hobnailed boots and a hat to last for the next twelve months. When it rained they would place a grain sack around their shoulders fixing the two corners with a six inch nail.

When we started growing corn again Dad hired grain sacks from the merchants: one of my jobs was to find these empty sacks so that they could be returned to stop the hire charge. It was a case of hunt the thimble because the men used to hide them away, but before the grain sacks were available our workman used to cut holes for his head and arms in a hessian bran sack, wearing it when it rained. If it was muggy day or misty with rain when we had to drive a cow to Titwell, or take sheep to Yanston for dipping, clouds of steam would be rising from him like a racehorse after a hard race by the time we got home. He mixed the pig food in a cut-in-half cider hogshead barrel, consisting of barley meal, bran and any vegetable waste surplus at the time, such as fallen apples, all mixed together with water. This time the bran sack would be fixed around his waist. There was a gap between the sack and his leggings which would accumulate easily an inch thick layer of fermenting pig food, and this remained until he changed his breeches on Saturday night!

But that was the way things were, hardly any of the houses in the village had water piped indoors. It all had to be carried either from the village well, or from the standpipe opposite the bakers. Daily personal hygiene was a chore; Saturday was bath night, Sunday change of clothes day, and Monday wash day. Mother used to provide a towel beside the pump outside the backdoor at Court Barton. The men were adept at pumping with one hand and putting their heads under the spout in summer, but gave it a miss in winter. She would grumble to Dad that all the dirt came off in the towel, especially at threshing time.

CHAPTER TWO

Village Life

Great Characters

There were great characters in the village of whom I became aware very early on. Even when in the pushchair I remember one man chasing another around a parked car with a carving knife. Whether I thought that normal behaviour I can't recall, perhaps I have gained my inhibitions since, or was it the love and protection I had at home which imprinted the incident to last in my memory a lifetime. It seemed as I got older that every out-of-the-ordinary male person had a nickname and I quickly learnt that the two men imprinted on my memory were cousins, both very eccentric, bordering on the loony.

Johnny Lugger

One, Johnny Lugger was married, the other 'Daddy Andrews' was single and as far as I remember they lived together. Johnny Lugger's wife played the piano every evening in their front room, and she had a repertoire of three notes going up the scale, which she played consecutively and continuously for hours on end, which drove the neighbours up the wall.

Johnny Lugger had a nickname tacked after his name which was a swear word to rhyme with Lugger. Whether that was to do with his volatile and sometimes violent temper I cannot recall, but I know it was manna from heaven to us boys, a swear word that could almost be used with impunity, if not in front of our parents. It was on our lips every time someone mentioned his behaviour, which was often. He would be leaning against his front door post every time we passed to catch the bus for school at the Post Office. Acutely aware that he must not be offended, we would dutifully say:

"Good Morning Mr Lugger"

It was with the greatest difficulty we omitted the offending word because it was on our lips so much.

Now the word 'lidegert' was used a lot in relation to fish. I have searched books on the dialect by Clement Martin and Jan Stewer but they make no mention of it, yet Harold Horton, a school master and renowned raconteur of the dialect said he had heard the word used in Plymouth fish market. Filthy great or "fulty gert" meant huge but a lidegert was bigger than that. John Wyatt caught a conger eel from the little bridge over Parson's Brook. I can see it now curled several times around the bottom of a ten gallon churn still wriggling although its head was cut off. That according to John was a "gert lidegert."

Jim Warren was leaning over the same bridge one evening. A combination of floodwater after heavy rain and an exceptional high tide had turned the brook into a small river, yet surprisingly the water was clear enough to see to the bottom. He was idly watching small trout making their way upstream when suddenly three large sea trout swam into view, obviously they had taken the wrong course up the river. Glancing over his shoulder and barely taking his eyes off the fish, he saw Johnny Lugger coming along the footpath carrying a net; forgetting all word discipline in his excitement, he called out:

"Quick, quick, quick, Mr Johnny Lugger B ------ three fulty gert lidegerts."

Daddy Andrews

Daddy Andrews possessed a frock coat and top hat, which he paraded through the village on occasion if the policeman was absent, maybe he imagined himself a defender of the law. My mother told me this story. The local salmon poacher, hearing the policeman was otherwise engaged at the magistrates' court in Kingsbridge and knowing there was a full tide with plenty of river water to meet it, decided that conditions were just right for a salmon run and to try his luck with a spear at the weir. Daddy Andrews on hearing of his intentions decided to make every effort to prevent him, so he donned top hat, tails and dark trousers and hurried to the gateway in the middle of Linkham Lake Hill which overlooked the weir. Standing on the gate as far up as he could without toppling over, he shouted. The poacher looking up against the sun thought the policeman had returned early, and grabbing his still empty net and spear he made his escape across the slippery stones to the Venn side of the river, falling in twice.

The Blacksmith

The blacksmith was called "Lekatere". I never could think why until I took a horse down to be shod one day when I was quite young. I was fascinated with his skill. He made the shoes from ten foot lengths of iron rods, cutting the length of the shoe off, heating the iron, and then bending the iron around the anvil to the shape of the shoe. He then burned it into the hoof to make sure it fitted because every hoof was a different size and shape' and finally made the holes for the nails. Modern farriers use ready made shoes. I must have asked him questions which he was kind enough to explain. When describing a method or what he was doing, he would say very quickly, "like that there" and it really did sound like "lekatere". He must have been very talented because he took to repairing cars; maybe it was a lot pleasanter to peer under a bonnet than lift a huge shire's foot. In the end there was a conflict of interest, I remember our workman telling Dad,

"Lekatere can't shoe the 'oss today because 'ees got a car to do".

Eventually we went to the blacksmith at Churchstow.

The Wheelwright

It must have been ten years before that I watched the blacksmith and the wheelwright, who had a workshop just a few yards farther up the road, bond a cart or maybe a wagon wheel down by the stream (Parson's Brook before it hits the river). The blacksmith had made the rim and the wheelwright the wheel. I am sure I remember seeing older boys trundling them down to the stream, on second thoughts it could have been apprentices. Anyway they had a wood fire to heat the rim to expand it, then it was hammered on to the wheel, finally buckets of water were thrown over the wheel to shrink the rim. I suspect I would have been in a pushchair because my nanny lived very close, but I remember very clearly the clouds of steam rising into the air. The blacksmith made iron hoops for a few pence for boys to trundle with the aid of an iron hook; likewise the wheelwright would allow boys to make trolleys from waste wood which was fixed on old pram wheels and axles. The trolleys were the transport for the materials for bonfire night.

Nicknames

Another nice chap had a terrible stammer and every sentence was punctuated with "fer" which seemed to help his stammer: he seemed completely unselfconscious about it and would stamp his foot until he got the sentence out. He was known as "Fer Whether or No" as he often said it. There were always competitions for something or other. It might be the biggest leek one year or the biggest potato and usually judged by the pub landlady. One year it was for the earliest crop of potatoes of a certain size. "Fer Whether or No" decided to chit his potatoes under his bed to get an early crop. When asked in the spring how his potatoes were doing he replied:

"I fer forgot all about 'em! And they fer grew right up through the fer mattress."

I remember he and another farmer had a long and heated argument about the scum which forms in the centre of the river with the incoming tide. The other farmer reckoned it heralded a fine spell of weather, "Fer Whether or No" said it couldn't possibly be,

"Because I have seen it fer 'undreds of times and us don't get that amount of fer fine weather."

My nickname was 'Froggy,' 'the frog', or 'you gert frog' if I annoyed someone. Only because when young I had (and still do), a fascination for spawn, tadpoles, frogs and toads. I took a frog to school in my coat pocket for a nature study lesson once and was evermore labelled. Nicknames were handed down from father to son, there were three generations of 'Pincher' Moores but not always the firstborn inherited the title.

I have to jump about twenty years for the next nickname. Sid Edgecombe, a much respected stonemason and my hero of Dunkirk, was recounting his day's experience one Friday evening in the pub. He had asked the lady of the house where he was working that day, if she could heat his pasty in the Aga stove for his dinner. When she opened the oven door, alas her much loved cat was curled up inside.

"Was 'er daid?" asked an innocent listener. He was known as 'Waserdaid' until the day he died.

Nicknames, like so many of the families which lived in the village for nearly a century or more, have dispersed with the coming of the motor car. One house in the village which housed three generations to my knowledge was sold in the late 1960s when the last member passed on. It then changed hands four times in five years. I was talking to an Aveton Gifford girl, now like me getting on in years, only a week or so ago who said:

"When I was a girl you could walk along the street and know who lived in each house both sides, because they had been there for generations."

Drasher Bill

The area of the village from Tree Corner to the Rectory Gate was very dark at night even before the blackout of the war. Our Parish Councillor at Rural District Council level always voted against lamps along the street because it would put a penny on the rates. There were no lights from windows or doorways to alleviate the problem. I had joined the choir at eight years of age, choir practices were held in the rectory music room, and in winter I always hung around for an older member to appear before entering the dark drive up to the Rectory. There was always some boy ready to pounce out on a smaller, timid member from out of the rhododendron bushes which hemmed the drive on either side, thus frightening the living daylights out of any victim.

The Lord Nelson - Bill Elliott at the wheel, Bridge End c1912

Old Smokey Bill Dale lived at Challons Combe then, Smokey because he ran a steam engine and threshing tackle; most times an aroma of steam and coal smoke accompanied him. There was another Smokey Bill at the southern end of the village, but he drove a steam roller for the highway authority. If some differential was required one was Drasher Bill (Thresher Bill) and the other Steam Roller Bill.

Drasher Bill had long hair down to his shoulders with an equally long almost white beard. He rode a shoeless grey mare down to the pub; it was alright in daylight because one could see her coming, at night it was different. Why I stayed behind one choir practice night I cannot remember, perhaps I had to practice a solo. I was always extremely nervous with solos and needed encouragement, but loved singing. I could hit the high notes then. I was armed with a torch and there was a full moon, but a dense fog had descended on the valley casting an eerie sort of light. I ran down between the rhododendron bushes thinking I could hear footsteps and burst out into the road to nearly cannon into a grey, ghostly object on four legs. The mare shied and stopped dead, sending her rider across her neck hanging on for dear life, and hollering blue murder. I didn't wait to see if he was alright but legged it home quicker than I had ever done before. Smokey Bill got drunk in the Seven Stars one market day and asked for a haircut. His 'pals' fetched a set of horse clippers, cutting one stroke close to his head from ear to ear and another from neck to forehead, then sent him home.

The Horse Race

There was a story shrouded in the mists of time when I was a lad about a horse race. It was mentioned rarely except that it was between a landlord of the one of the pubs and the local rabbit trapper. In those days rabbits were unsaleable when there wasn't an R in the month. The trapper supplemented his income by keeping a few ponies down at Bantham and selling pony rides during the summer. I was beginning to think it really was a myth until several years ago my daughter did some gardening jobs for an ex-Aveton Gifford boy who lived at Buckland. He spoke of a two horse race between a hunter and a pony nearly two hands smaller over a distance of a little more than two miles. When he recalled that bets of five pounds were being placed, which was more than two weeks wages for a working man, my daughter was incredulous. Seeing her disbelief he said:

'Well! We had to provide our own entertainment then you know, and it kept us entertained for weeks."

I know only one fact and that is the small horse won. One can speculate on the course; was it down the tidal road, up by North Efford, Waterhead, Borough Lane, Ashford and then home, or up the Chantry road, Hoppy Green Lane, Linkham Lake Hill and home, or the reverse way in each case. Both were just about the right distance. Unfortunately the old man died before I got in touch. The rumour was, when I was young, that skulduggery took place; that a slippery substance was spread over the road where it cambered away sharply and the big horse slipped up giving the smaller horse the advantage. Well even today there is a place on each of those speculated courses where the road cambers sharply away. My mother could have given me the answer but she chose never to mention it. Was it because as a pillar of the Church and Mothers Union she dismissed the debauchery of the drinking and gambling completely from her mind?

Church and Chapel

Reverend Elston George Payne Rector of Aveton Gifford 1925-46

The Rector was a kindly little man, a very good sick visitor but a strict disciplinarian as far as we were concerned. I suppose he had to be. He told my mother when he first came to the village that he had been down to Waterhead Farm to try to get the owner to pay up his tithe[3] arrears. The reply referred to Mr Payne's predecessors,

"I didn't pay Pitman, I didn't pay Boultbee so I bain't going to pay you Payne."

He was keen to embrace the chapel in combined services although I never felt the members of the chapel reciprocated that much.

A school friend of mine went to chapel every Sunday night and we used to swap experiences on the way to school in Kingsbridge on Monday mornings, after all we had long enough. By the time the bus ground away in bottom gear up Aveton Gifford Hill and stopped at every farm along the route, a half hour had gone by. He was a marvellous mimic and I remember three of his reports in particular. We called the preachers Chapel Parsons or "Laukel Praichers" (Local Preachers). Most preached fire and brimstone, they came mainly from the farming community and some spoke in broad dialect. One or two were star attractions drawing a big congregation from far and wide. One Sunday evening the difficulty of a rich man entering the Kingdom Of Heaven was being expounded. After a moment's thought the preacher elaborated:

"Yer, it idden naw gude telling ee 'bout camels gwain dru hies of naedles, you ouldn't naw nort 'bout they. I'll put it lak this yer. Tis aizier fur th'ol cow to clammer up a gert helm tray an calvie in th'ol craw's nest than fur a raich man to git to Eben!

---

[3] The tithe was an annual payment of a proportion (originally one-tenth) of the yearly produce of the land, which was payable by parishioners to the parish church, to support it and its clergyman. Originally tithes were paid 'in kind' (wool, milk, honey, fish, barley etc) and were payable on 3 categories of produce:
- All things which grew and which increased annually e.g. grain, vegetables and wood.
- All things which were nourished by the ground, livestock and their produce like milk, hides, eggs and wool.
- The produce of man's labour – particularly the profits of mills and fishing. The payment of tithe was a cause of endless dispute between the tithe owners and the tithe payers – between clergy and parishioners. In addition, Quakers and other non-conformists objected to paying any tithes to support the established church. Tithing was seen as increasingly irrelevant to the needs of the community and the developing agricultural industry.

(It's no good telling you about camels going through eyes of needles, you would not know anything about them. I'll put it like this. It would be easier for a cow to clamber up a great elm tree and calve in a crow's nest than for a rich man to get to Heaven.)

On another occasion the preacher was giving dire warning on the evils of drinking alcohol; at the end of the sermon he cried:

"Bring it to me and I will throw it in the river."

Then announcing the last hymn.

"Y'mn nomber wan 'undred an' levon, wan, wan, wan. Dree wan's." (Hymn number 111. One, one, one. Three ones). *Down by the river."*

Weslyan Chapel, Fore Street. Early 1900's

Some preachers had a way of homing in on a member of the congregation and looking through the person like a laser beam. One Monday morning my pal was sorely troubled; the preacher was haranguing the congregation the evening before about the 'devil in our midst,' looking straight through my friend as he said it. The boy spoke as if ravaged by guilt.

"How the hell did he know I was pinching apples on Saturday afternoon?"

There were five shops in the village then, two of which were butchers. When one butcher retired the other butcher bought his shop and closed it down to avoid any incoming competition.

In the grocers' shops everything was stored in large containers and weighed off to the customers in small quantities.

When the telephone was brought from Loddiswell to the village the navvies were mainly Irishmen. A story going the rounds at the time was that an Irishman called into one of the shops for loose tobacco and was served. The next time he called in the shop was nearly full.

"A hounce of shag baccy please sorr' and keep your bleeding thumb off it this time."

The shopkeeper expostulated, but the customers all looked at one another nodding their heads.

A farmer from Waterhead helped Dad one day a week. He was to teach me when I got older how to drive horses and do other jobs about the farm. I will call him My Mentor. He was a widower and would have liked a son, so was very kind to me. We often had discussions. The ghost at South Efford had allegedly made an appearance recently so I asked him if it could be true.

"Ghosts! I don't set no store by they. But Tom, my next door neighbour, 'ee sees one every Saturday night an' 'its at 'in with 'is stick too."

He wasn't a churchgoer as far as I remember, except to funerals, but he objected to the idea of combined services with the chapel. He called them ranters.

We had a prolonged dry spell all through May and half way into June and grass for hay was almost non-existent. Hay was the staple winter feed then. The Rector called for a combined service of prayer for rain with the chapel. That Sunday night there was a terrific thunder storm which washed Tom's freshly sown turnips down into the road. I met My Mentor on the way to school next morning, he had run out of fags and was about to enter the shop. He had seen the mess of his neighbour's turnips and when I told him about the combined prayer for rain, he glanced up the road towards the chapel with dark threatening looks.

"They Ranters!"

Fireworks

Guy Fawkes night was looked forward to by the village boys from one year to the next. For weeks beforehand they would be gathering combustible material for a huge bonfire on the marsh. Fireworks were freely available. Maybe there was a restriction on the very young buying them, but I had no difficulty that I remember; my school pal had an aunt who ran a newspaper shop in Kingsbridge which also sold fireworks, probably that helped. A penny demon banger would open an unlocked front door if placed under the weather board. It must have been bad for the human occupants but what it did to the dogs and cats I cannot imagine. Fireworks night would end with the two ends of the village forming separate groups on either side of the bonfire and throwing fireworks at each other. In 1938 my brother who was in the Metropolitan Police brought down fireworks which we had the night before the official day because he had to return to London the next day. They were of a quality I had not seen, rockets full of stars, Roman candles and huge Catherine wheels, a truly memorable occasion. I had two firework nights that year; I don't think anyone would have guessed that we would see no more for six long years.

Gas Masks

We had all been given gas masks. On one or two occasions we had to take them to school to practice putting them on. Each gas mask was contained in a square, cardboard box supported by a flimsy piece of string to encircle one's neck. Some found them useful as a means of defence, others tried to play conkers with them. My mentor took one look at my gas mask and severely harangued Neville Chamberlain.

"'Ee's giving you bl --- y gas masks while 'itlers building tanks".

Dad was more complacent surprisingly, and said to take no notice. Britain needed time to build tanks too.

It is always said one remembers exactly where one was on a momentous occasion. I had been to church on that September morning in 1939, and was running to the village on an errand of which I do not have the foggiest notion now. As I ran around Tree Corner I met Jim Warren, he was quite a bit older than me, wearing a worried expression and striding purposely towards Waterhead. He did not slacken his pace but called out:

"Quick! Get your gas mask Froggy, war has been declared."

I remember being rooted to the spot for several minutes wondering whether to go back home or finish my errand. I think I finished my errand.

Children practising wearing gas masks

CHAPTER THREE

The War

The war came with its directives, regulations and capital letters which were to change the face of agriculture in this country for ever. First we had to learn the names of the various ruling bodies referred to us by their initials or abbreviations. War Ag was for the War Agricultural Council, MoF for Ministry of Food, MoWP for Ministry of War Production and so on. WAEC was the War Agricultural Executive Committee with an office in every district based on the District Council area. The WAEC consisted of a man from the Ministry of Agriculture in charge of a committee of mainly retired farmers who visited each farm and told them how many acres of this and that to grow. We had to grow grain and potatoes and only had the necessary machinery for an all-grass farm. We hired a contractor to do the ploughing and had to borrow machinery or hire it from a government run machinery depot.

We quickly became aware of the horrors of war with the sinking of HMS Courageous off the Devon coast just six weeks into the conflict. One survivor went home to Kingsbridge on our school bus and kept jumping off to be sick every time we stopped; we were told he had swallowed sea water. After that we hardly knew a war was on for the next eight months. We were urged to grow more food. Areas which had become gorse, bramble and bracken were ploughed up and reseeded despite their quite hazardous steepness. There were slogans like "Dig for victory", "Make two blades of grass grow where one grew before", "Drain that swamp" etc, as well as the various posters on the "Careless talk costs lives" theme.

Brand names disappeared, there was only one brand of beer, cider was scrumpy and only one brand of petrol named Pool. The Rector, who was very good at giving people lifts, disliked Pool petrol intensely because it was far inferior to the brand he had always used and was always moaning that his car hardly climbed Kingsbridge Hill on it.

Nettles and Mushrooms

Food became scarce. Nettles we were told are very rich in vitamin A and C, although each leaf is covered by stinging hairs which are in fact a hollow tube containing formic acid and an enzyme; the acid caused the burning sensation on one's skin and the enzyme produced the white blister. The formic acid would be destroyed by cooking and the end result would be equivalent to spinach. One could make nettle tea, it could be used cold as a lotion, one could make nettle soup or wine, mix it with cream or milk for creamed nettles or sugar for nettle syrup. Ninety tons said the leaflet had been gathered by the County Herb Committees. Full of patriotic fervour and suitably kitted out with gauntlets, I sallied forth in search of young nettles for the creamed nettle recipe. We only had them once. The same thing happened with dandelions.

Mushrooms were abundant; they even came up in the corn crops from the old turf we had ploughed in. I must have mistaken the Yellow Stainer variety *(Agaricus xanthodermus)* for the Horse Mushroom *(Agaricus arvensis)* and was violently sick. To this day I cannot bear the smell of mushrooms frying let alone eating them. Giant puffballs are edible too but I preferred to kick them when ripe to see the yellow-brown spores cloud up to the sky.

Ministry Drainage Schemes

A Ministry scheme to drain wet areas was set up. Dad joined this one because he did not like rushes, and in each of the two valleys on our farm there were several overflowing springs in the hillsides creating a bog covered in rush and wild iris. Our work was done by hand, finding the old stone drains laid in the last century and replacing them with new earthenware drains. Most were choked, but some had been destroyed by the craze for 'drowning' at the turn of the century. Drowning was a means of producing early grass through a system of irrigation channels cut horizontally from a spring in the hillside to allow water to run over the pasture downhill. I was told it produced lush, valueless grass because it leached out any nitrogen in the soil and the practice died a natural death.

There were three men digging, one was the foreman who became as excited as a child when he found an old drain, two were ex-unemployed men who had to do some form of war work. It was an uncomfortable job with feet continually in water, wet trousers from the muddy sides of the trenches they dug, and hard work cutting through the rushes. Dad would visit them every day, sometimes I would go with him. One man was totally unsuited for the work; he would have found brushing a smooth concrete floor beyond him. After watching him for a while Dad turned to me with a quote from the bible,

"I cannot dig, to beg I am ashamed."

I asked a skilled self-employed farm worker many years later what he thought of farmers visiting him on the job which at times could be at the farthest end of the property. His thoughts intrigued me. If a farmer did not bother to visit once a day then he would appear disinterested in the man's work and border on the insulting. If he visited more than once a day then it would question the man's integrity to do a fair day's work and a first class job.

Dunkirk

After Dunkirk the war hit us. I was waiting for the bus when Sid Edgecombe came along to catch it; he was in full army uniform but didn't carry a rifle. It may seem odd now but at that time every soldier I saw carried his rifle everywhere, and stupidly boy-like I asked him where it was:

"In Dunkirk harbour," was his reply.

I was overawed and tongue-tied to be in the presence of a hero. I wanted to ask him what his experiences were, how he managed to get away, but I was dumbstruck and said nothing.

Billets, Bagpipes and Elephants

By the end of July soldiers were everywhere, it was a brilliant summer and everyone thought the Germans would invade. The Northumberland Fusiliers were billeted in the village school. All the village girls were kept indoors or escorted everywhere by their mothers. The soldiers kept asking the boys if they had any sisters and if so 'what are they doing toneet.' The boys could not understand a word they were saying and teased them mercilessly for the way they talked. The Black Watch were stationed in the Albion Hotel in Kingsbridge and when they marched along the quay with their bagpipes, fifes and drums playing "Over The Sea To Skye" it made every schoolboy want to run away and join the army. The girls would follow along after them trying to get their skirts to swing from side to side like the soldiers kilts. There was a contingent of Indian troops complete with elephants in the goods section of the Kingsbridge railway yard: we often met them in the school dinner break exercising the elephants. I couldn't imagine what use they would have in warfare, but my school pal would get quite excited at the size of their spoor, and would track along behind them, no doubt imagining himself on a big game hunt. When the threat of invasion receded due to the heroic bravery of the RAF, the soldiers left.

The Searchlight Battery

We were designated a night fighter area in the air defence of Plymouth and told that a searchlight battery was to be installed on the farm. My parents could not have refused if they wanted to. This consisted of three searchlights, seven corrugated iron huts, one a cook house, and a company of men with a captain in command. It was built by the

Pioneer Corps and occupied by men from the Royal Artillery. To provide the power for the lights two massive generators were placed in the road beside the site. After a while the soldiers integrated well with the village people and provided a source of skilled casual labour for the farms as quite a few were gardeners and farm workers. There were a few camp followers, single girls, lonely young women whose husbands were away, and a dog.

David with Flo and Bruce in 1940

The dog used to come with me rabbiting. He was extremely clever at digging out a laid up ferret, it saved me hours of hanging around waiting for the ferret to have its fill on the rabbit it had killed. Dad had bought me a dozen ewes and a sheepdog pup for me to train when I was twelve. I was told never to take her rabbiting until she was older, she had to learn her trade first. It was uncanny, how the camp dog would always find me wherever and whenever I was rabbiting.

I remember working in a field of hay beside the site with My Mentor. It must have been in the evening after school, cocking up the hay because it was not fit to carry, and it was going to rain. This was common practice then; it was really making miniature ricks, rounded at the top with scraped sides to allow the rain to run off without damaging the hay. A handsome young bombardier with an Errol Flynn moustache sauntered up to inspect the work we were doing, casually he said:

"There will be several bum 'oles in them tonight."

My companion burst out laughing and I was inwardly incensed that my neat handiwork should be thus desecrated, but when we came to pick up the hay cocks two weeks later, although a bit shrunk through natural settling they were otherwise untouched and very good hay. I had a lot to learn about cockney humour.

A Czechoslovakian woman had come to stay with her children. She was well educated, extremely pleasant and escaped to England with her husband when her country was invaded by the Germans. She used to buy eggs from mother at the door but had a strong accent. When the bombing of Plymouth started I was shocked to hear she had been accused of signalling to passing German planes: the harassment was so intense she went back to London.

Egg Production

Mother was in charge of egg production, Dad and I did the donkey work. Being free range the hens would not all go in their respective houses until almost dark. Double summer time came into being early in the war, so that meant the hens would not go to bed until nearly midnight; I did hurry them up a little by training my little dog to round up the stragglers. She was allowed to give the last one in the pophole a poke up the backside. Double summer time was a real hardship to farmers, as it meant the dew did not burn off the hay or corn till late in the morning, meaning harvesting could not start till after noon. One bright politician suggested farmers should work to a different time, so we tried it for a while but it was impossible. For example a milk lorry driver had to work to the factory time table not to a farm's time: markets had to keep to slaughterhouse time. In the end we just worked longer hours.

Rural life continued much the same as it always had. Evacuees from London had been absorbed reasonably well in the village. The egg cases were picked up every Tuesday, the van driver brought the cash for the last week's pickup. Mother would study the returns and if there were more cracked eggs than she thought there ought to have been, she would have a go at the van driver for not driving carefully enough:

"No it isn't that at all Ma'am, I graded them myself and the shells were awful thin."

Then she would have at go at Dad saying he wasn't supervising the mixing of the food, that the right amount of calcium must have been omitted. Or another time it would be me not being careful enough gathering the eggs.

We mixed our own poultry and cow feed on the floor of the barn, as well as the fertiliser for the various crops, because it was so much cheaper to buy straights. We mixed super phosphate, muriate of potash and nitrogen for each crop. For instance, potatoes would have 5cwt of potash, 3cwt of phosphate and 2cwt of nitrogen per acre and barley would have 3cwt of phosphate, 2cwt of nitrogen and I cwt of potash per acre.

First Aid !

As well as initials for agriculture, we had them in day to day life as well. ARP for Air Raid Precautions, LDV for Local Defence Volunteers later to become the Home Guard. As well as working twelve hours a day in the fields, farmers and farmworkers had to join one of these organisations. We had demonstrations showing us how to put out an incendiary bomb by using a very long handled shovel and covering it with sand. There were First Aid classes, make do and mend, even how to use a rifle, although there were no rifles as those lost in Dunkirk harbour had not been replaced yet.

I remember a school pal and I were asked to be the casualties at a First Aid examination in the village school. The local butcher, a big burly man, amongst others was to be examined. In those days artificial respiration was done with the patient lying on his or her tummy, with the person doing the reviving expelling the lungs by pressing down on the back of the chest to the count of four and letting the lungs refill also to the count of four. I was lying on my back when the butcher came in, having had all of my limbs 'broken', my head in a splint and my body bandaged up like a mummy by previous students. The butcher was told to give me artificial respiration by the examining doctor. The butcher looked down at me and said:

"Turn over." I dutifully started to roll over.

"Oh no you don't," said the doctor, *"Do it properly".*

The butcher got down on his knees and carefully crossed one arm and one leg in the direction he was to turn me and gently rolled me over, placing both arms in the correct position and my head on one side. He expelled my lungs to the count of four. He bore down on me with such strength I thought he had broken my ribs; for days after they were sore. I think they all passed that night. I especially remember a seventeen year old farmer's daughter from Churchstow parish. As she left the room the doctor said to me:

"My word she is good! Who is she?"

I was so proud to be able to tell him. She became a nurse and went on to become matron of a big London hospital. A wealthy lady had organised the event and I can see my pal's face now as she handed us a one pound note each at the end of the evening.

Bicycle Accident

There was an old chap in the village who once worked for Dad, he was getting on now and crippled with arthritis but was able to look after the baker's pigs. Although almost illiterate he could work out exactly when a sow would farrow from the time she went to the boar. Whenever I saw him feeding the fattening pigs he wore a top hat and tail coat, using colourful language the whole time. He lived about forty paces from The Commercial on the other side of the street and on his frequent journeys to the pub would lean heavily on two sticks; the point on which they touched the ground would be at least two paces from his feet. Walking diagonally across the road for his nightly sustenance he would be in the middle of the road for a very long time. I must have been coming back from the pictures about closing time one night on my bike in the blackout when I hit him. In mitigation I will say one could not see a thing with the lights then as they were masked allowing only a pinpoint of light to fall on the ground just ahead. Maybe the battery was a bit low, but I hit him. He lay on the ground moaning and there was a slight cut on his bald head. After accusing me of going too fast he went silent.

I know now that he had fallen asleep. His daughter, who had the dubious pleasure of looking after him rushed out and surveyed the old man prostrate on the ground.

"You've killed 'im."

With a sort of snore the old man stirred, his daughter picked him up threatening all sorts of legal action and escorted him indoors. I must have been in a high state of anxiety when I arrived home, not knowing if I was going to be had for speeding or manslaughter. Dad told me not to worry, he would sort it out in the morning, and not to be late getting the cows in next day. When I got in for breakfast from milking Dad had already sorted it out.

"Oh I gave his daughter a ten bob note (50p) and told her to keep the old man in bed for a day or two".

I was quite famous for a couple of weeks for knocking the old man's sticks away without hurting him.

The Home Guard

As the desert campaign progressed in North Africa a weapon called a spicket mortar had proved successful and the Aveton Gifford Company was allocated one of these. Our superiors deemed it necessary to practice with it away from the public eye and chose the top of Pittons as an appropriate place.

It was cumbersome and heavy, taking four men to carry it and two to carry the bomb. We were supposed to march in step up the steepest part of Pittons to the top, fire it once and march back down again. Our boots were polished for parading, the hill was incredibly steep and always slippery, so we fell flat on our faces going up and slipped on our backsides coming down.

Those members of the farming community who joined the Home Guard and were compelled to attend two training sessions a week found it boring and extremely irksome. As the war progressed pitchforks, or prangs as we called them, were replaced by rifles.

Drilling and stripping of weaponry, together with target shooting with live ammunition and the discipline needed for the protection of colleagues was accepted as part of the job we were called upon to do. But I felt as a very young recruit that there were too many chiefs and not enough Indians. All those who had served in the Great War were made sergeants and there were many of them.

Fred Edgecombe senior - one of the first to join the LDV

Then there was the observation post at Harraton Cross which had to be manned all night and every night, the object was I suppose to look out for enemy parachutists and report on any bombs being dropped. I only went there on a couple of occasions and had great difficulty keeping awake after a hard day's work. The talking point for almost a year was when the guards were visited by a drunken commander in the middle of an air raid on Plymouth with the words:

"Did you 'ear that bomb drop."

Then there were pointless exercises when one platoon would go off into the night and another platoon was sent to find them. On one occasion the second platoon had as its tracker a tough farmer's son from Staunton. He quickly located the first platoon in a barn at Ashford under a heap of loose hay, fixing his bayonet to his rifle he started to prod the hay, whereupon the whole of the platoon emerged with their hands up. They were disarmed and marched back as prisoners to the HQ much earlier than expected, to find their commanders had retreated to the pub. Yet I have no doubt that every man would have fought to his last drop of blood had they been called upon to do so.

Plymouth Bombed

We could only watch the bombing of Plymouth with sorrow for the inhabitants and anger at the German planes above us. Occasionally a Heinkel would get caught in the searchlight beam and passed from one beam to another, and there were searchlights dotted about all over the South Hams. One night a German plane jettisoned its cargo when it had a British night fighter on its tail. One bomb dropped in a field above the village, one behind Pittons and the other over at Pond Farm. I happened to see the sparks as the bombs left the bomb rack. Another night a bomb blew out the bank of the regatta marshes below the bridge and flooded an area the size of a small farm. It took years to repair the sea wall effectively.

After the last big raid on Plymouth German tactics seemed to change, and there followed hit and run raids throughout the South Hams which affected all of us. Mother used to order her groceries once a week from a shop in Kingsbridge. Their representative would call on a Wednesday and their van would deliver on Friday. I can see mother now carefully cutting out the coupons for the groceries from the ration books on to the kitchen table with the kitchen scissors. He was originally from Aveton Gifford and was known to Mum and Dad from a boy. They looked forward to his coming because he went round all the farms and kept them abreast of the news. His wife worked in a butcher's shop in Kingsbridge. In the first raid on the town the shop received a direct hit. Her body was thrown up on the roof of the bank next door. We never saw him again.

My Mentor Marries

It was about this time that my father took me aside one day and told me 'My Mentor' was getting married again to a spinster from Loddiswell who, as my father put it, was a devout chapel goer, in fact he thought she must be a little touched as she was quite convinced she had seen the Lord. I remember this troubled me greatly, because I was very fond of my old friend and knew at first hand his opinion of 'Ranters'. I just could not see how they could get along and must have voiced my fears. I remember Dad saying:

"Look Son! He has been a widower for nine years, he must get very lonely and she is no chicken either. I think it will work out alright."

I still had grave doubts but in the end Dad was right as usual.

David 1942

My Brother

At the end of 1942 I left school. My brother had been killed in September returning from a night bombing raid on Bremen. I had worshipped him. I looked forward so much to his coming home on each leave and now he was buried in foreign soil. I just wanted to do as much as I could for my country to avenge my beloved hero's death if possible; to me school was a waste of time and Dad needed me at home desperately.

Old Skills

I was quite skilled in everyday farm work but Dad decided I should learn the old skills, so I was sent to work with My Mentor for two or three days a week. He in turn returned my labour on our farm. He taught me how to use a flail for threshing sheaves; a cumbersome piece of wood similar to a baseball bat but twice as thick and heavy, it was attached to a six foot long handle by a piece of leather, actually a piece of old boot, and the flail was swung around the head to fall flat on the ears of grain. If the swing was imperfect, a blow to the back of the head would quickly lead to perfection in your own interest. I was taught to thatch, to make rope from straw to keep the thatch on, to make spears from hazel boughs to keep the rope on, to turf hedge, to erect a stone wall of quoins and shiners, the Devon way, the Cornish way and a hundred other names and methods.

He taught me to 'dray foyer' it is the nearest spelling I can get to the sound as I have never seen the word in print, and guess it is a corruption of the word furrow and dray was to carry or pull. Three furrows were taken out at the bottom of the field to be ploughed, then using a scoop like a giant fire shovel the horseman collected a load of earth and drove it to the top of the field. As it was tipped it spread the earth, and then the process continued until all the ploughed earth was cleared. This was the means to counteract erosion as the fields were all ploughed downhill.

He was a brilliant horseman, not only did he teach me how to plough, work the ground down and drill root seed as straight as a die for accurate horse hoeing, but also how to care for their needs. He taught me how to stop them if they ran away, something I never expected to have to do, yet was thrown into the situation within two months. He was a good dog handler as well. I had a young dog which I was training at the time and I remember his exact words:

"Send her up around the biggest, steepest field you've got. By the time she gets to the top she will be out of breath and will not start to bite and be glad to stop".

In one sentence he hit on the two biggest problems with a young sheepdog. Because they have an inbred killer instinct it is difficult to stop them, and keep them far enough yet not too far off the sheep.

The Storyteller

He was a fascinating storyteller, describing the various village outings by boat in the days before the charabanc[4]. He said he only went on a charabanc outing once with Anthony Luscombe who kept his bus at Endsleigh Place (for some reason it was known to us as Beelzebub's Castle). It was the usual run, Plymouth, via Princetown, Ashburton's Lion Hotel and home. There was a peculiar fascination with the drab, grey buildings of the prison which were usually shrouded in mist, and if a working party of prisoners were seen a good time was had by all. It must have been something to do with 'there but for the grace of God go I', syndrome. Anthony never drove faster than twelve miles an hour, and on the moor's narrow roads considerably less. Reports suggested that it was My Mentor who got fed up with this, no doubt thinking of the cows he had to milk when he got home, but someone called out from the back of the bus:

"Antney dolee pull over, there's an 'oss 'an cart wants to pass."

---

[4] Early form of motor coach

Wesleyan Chapel Outing Aveton Gifford 1927

He spoke of ploughing matches and other competitions, warning me never to drink cider if I was competing, as the drink could be easily spiked with a diarrhoea inducing agent, then gave graphic details of those who had succumbed. Tales of farming when he was a boy, when sheep dips were mounted on a horse wagon. The sheep had to be pushed up a ramp on to the wagon, pushed into the dip, and when they came out on the other side were held by two men on either side to let the excess liquid drain back into the dip. A filthy job he conceded, one he avoided by pushing up the sheep at the other end. Sometimes a sheep would shake its fleece like a dog, drenching the men with dip. They were using arsenic based dips then as we all were doing until recent years when dips became based on organophosphorous compounds. I asked him if the men came to any harm.

"No!" he said, *"Only a bit yellow at the end of the day."*

Even now I don't know if the yellowness came from the arsenic or the colouring they put in the dip to smarten up the sheep a bit.

Every farm kept poultry of one sort or another then and as his farm bordered the estuary he kept geese to utilise the grass on the flats between tides. They were originally Embden cross Toulouse, but had stabilised into a breed of its own called the South Hams. In ninety five per cent of the geese males came white and the females coloured. His neighbour down the river bought a beautiful white gander of which he was justly proud, but began to get concerned in February at mating time as he had not seen the gander do anything. His fears were confirmed one month later when he found his prize gander sitting on a nest laying an egg. A whole year's gosling production down the drain! I was taught how to sex geese without suffering permanent damage from their wings.

Apple Tart and Clotted Cream

I had started taking my dinner but after a while his wife invited me to have the meal with them. She was a marvellous cook and probably the most saintly person I have ever met. She would say grace before each meal and as she was praying her husband would be stirring sugar into his hot tea and just as she was about to say Amen he would place his very hot spoon on the back of her hand. On another occasion she was elaborating on the marvellous preacher they had at chapel the night before and how he had lined them all up to shake their hands.

"Yes my dear, and did he tickle the palm of your hand with his forefinger."

To him it was only teasing, to my young mind it was sinfully hurtful, but she just smiled. They kept a couple of Guernseys which she milked and, as my mother did ten years before turned the milk into cream, butter and cheese. But after allowing the cream to rise she scalded the pan over the log fire in the hearth, not on the stove which would have been easier, this gave the cream a slightly smokey, superb, indescribable flavour when skimmed. Her apple tart was out of this world too and when she served it with a large dollop of clotted cream .... cor! The apples came from a small orchard a bit beyond the house. My Mentor was very proud of this orchard though he had little to do with it because it was planted by his predecessor who grew young trees for sale. There was every variety under the sun; Beauty of Bath, Devon Qualander (a crimson coloured apple with pink flesh), Allington Permain, Newton Wonder, Ellisons Orange and three sorts of russets of which Egremont was the best. Yes! I tried them all. He was very proud of his Ellisons Orange. He took an apple in to Kingsbridge for the horticultural expert to comment on. The verdict:

"What a big, beautiful apple. Do you mind if I taste 'in."

Then: *"Oh! you've lost the flavour by growing it on a gert big standard when it should be grown on a bush."*

I don't think he was too pleased with the comment.

Cider Making

The cider orchard was farther up the valley. He pounded his own cider apples by hand with a machine very like a root cutter but it was not as hard work because the apples were soft. I would sooner pound the apples than pick them up as I was always extremely sensitive to stinging nettles and nettles loved the shade of apple trees. It would have been incorrect to wear gloves then, one was supposed to get one's hands so hard as not to be bothered by thistles or nettles.

As I pounded the apples so he would lay the pulp in a six foot square box, layered by wheat straw to make an envelope placed under a twin screw press, which he reckoned was hundreds of years old. The envelopes would be a foot thick when covered with the straw, and the process was repeated gradually building up the envelopes upon one another up to the press. Long before the press was started juice would be pouring out of the envelopes and running along the stone channel into a granite trough. The juice was taken out by bucket and poured through a sieve into the hogsheads. I don't suppose he knew anything about yeast, tannin, enzymes and sugar but apple varieties vary in these contents, he just knew which varieties to use, the knowledge being handed down from generation to generation. After a few days the barrels would start to ferment and foaming froth would run down over the sides.

Cider making in the 21st century at Grove Park Farm, Aveton Gifford

He would check the barrels every day and top them up to prevent air getting in the barrels which would have turned the liquid to vinegar. The fermenting process went on for about four months when he would bung up the barrels with a little ceremony with a few friends. Before he got married the prettiest young woman in the hamlet would draw the first pint. I was never offered a drink because of my age but he promised to give me a drink on the day I told him I was getting married. Unfortunately he retired before then.

Straying away from cider for a moment I saw him make our first land girl 'hay sweet' one haymaking tea time. He took a twist of hay from the rick, wound it into a crown, placed it on her head then gave her the sweetest of kisses, and then tucked the crown back into the rick. It was a charming little ceremony never to be forgotten and looked back on with great nostalgia when baling took the romance out of haymaking.

Christmas Cider

He kept a special barrel just inside the door of the cellar which he topped up every Christmas with a bottle of whisky and a bottle of rum. This must have been standard practice because during the war our accountant told of a visit to a farm for the annual audit. The lane to the farm was pitted with boulders and three quarters of a mile long. He had a posh car, as most accountants seem to possess, and did not take it down the lane. It was a hot day, the lane was very dusty and the farmer offered him a jar of cider when he got to the house which he sank gratefully. He had to go back the next day because he could not read his figures, and enquired what on earth was in the cider: the reply was that the cider was ten years old and had been laced every Christmas with whisky and rum. Nowadays cider makers use sterile hessian bags for the envelopes because they say sprays have contaminated the wheat straw, but wheat straw today has neither the length nor strength to do the job. Incidentally I read last week that there is written evidence that Somerset cider makers added sugar to bottled cider early in the last century to produce cider with bubbles in it a good thirty years before the French 'learned' how to make champagne. They wouldn't have pinched the idea from us would they?

There was a small nursery on the east side of Waterhead beside the brook. I could never understand why the young trees were so bent until my mother said the previous owner Mr Davey was a cripple and used to crawl through the nursery and bend the young trees over to prune them. I presume the ground was too wet to carry a wheelchair. On his death he left his farm into a trust fund to support any cripple in the parish. My father was a trustee. There was only one who needed support when I was young, a woman called Gertie Wakeham, who lived with her father in the row of cottages next to the Commercial Inn. Those cottages were demolished by the blitz and never rebuilt. Gertie had polio as a child and wore callipers. I used to go to her father for a haircut and she would hold a candle close to my head so her father could see. I wasn't too keen on the exercise as the clippers were blunt and pulled my hair, while the other boys would tease me saying he must have put a pudding basin over my head and clipped underneath it. When Gertie died the Davey Trust was wound up and the money left over was put into another charity.

Cider apples fetched the dizzy heights of nearly £20 a ton during the war. Later in 1948 I decided to make up the lost trees at Court Barton with young trees from this nursery, but as soon as they started to crop they bent over worse than ever with the weight of the apples, and eventually snapped halfway up the trunk. Most farm orchards held forty trees and a tenant would have to pay compensation for lost trees on quitting the farm.

At times the civilian population was very short of food, but farmers were lucky enough to be able to augment the shortage, although they had to get a permit to be able to kill an animal. The butcher arrived at My Mentor's house one Saturday morning with Argentinean corned beef.

"You take that back to the village for Tommy Luckraft, 'ee voted for it all these years now 'ee can ate it."

Duck Shooting by Moonlight

There was a full moon and the wild ducks were pitching into My Mentor's barley and spoiling more than they were eating. It was illegal to discharge a gun after dusk but that didn't concern him over much, a duck would be better than corned beef. He crept up beside the hedge to face the moon, and as the ducks rose and crossed the moon's path he got two with a right and left barrel. Safely back in bed his wife said:

"Look there's a light."

"Yeh! Moonlight, I've just been out in it."

She pointed, *"No! Look! Up there on the ceiling."*

Seeing the pinpoint of a torch through the window on to the ceiling he slipped out of bed to see the policeman going out the yard gate. The law must have heard the shots and guessed correctly who had discharged them and shone his torch to see if the blinds were drawn. I suppose if there was a light showing the policeman would have had an excuse to search.

Badgers

My Mentor farmed at Stadbury before Waterhead. There were only three badger setts in the parish then, one at Torr Plantation, one at Chantry, the other in Stadbury Woods. Once a year the village organised a badger dig at Stadbury, complete with a cider barrel and baskets of bread and cheese for the midday break on a cart. He described the events in memorable detail. The head digger was a countryman of exceptional skill, and he had a biblical forename but for identification in this account I will call him Noah Parsons. He was as adept at snaring a salmon as he was at catching rabbits, foxes or digging out a badger, and was looked upon as a pariah by the river owners and fly fishermen, some of whom were on the magistrates' bench.

Badger dig at Stadbury. February 1921

If he got caught by the water bailiff and came before the bench he would be fined the maximum. Always asking for time to pay, he reckoned to be able reimburse the fine the next evening, or certainly by the next court if he knew the bailiff would be otherwise engaged giving evidence against another poacher. I asked him years later who were his regular customers, and he told me a few with the proviso:

"I can tell 'ee now cos they'm daid."

One name was a magistrate in another police authority, the others were as mind-boggling. Yet having relieved an otter of its fresh kill at Hatch Bridge when I was a lad, I fully understood their desire. I can tell you without hesitation that there is nothing in the culinary world like a fresh run salmon. It was not the magistrates' courts that ended Noah's salmon days, but a bacterial fungal disease called saprolegnia (cotton fungus which infects river weed and fish).

I seem to have strayed from the badger dig. Noah was merry but not drunk.He had dug down to the badger, and was carefully trying to fix an iron shackle to a back leg, and now and then he would hold up a handful of bristles to My Mentor asking if a shaving brush was required. When the badger had been dug out one unfortunate animal would be taken off to a barn for young terriers to be initiated into the art of 'holing it up.' On one occasion the badger escaped, ran down to the river, and swam across to the other side with the tide in. It must have been a memorable sight: a crowd of men at the water's edge, frustrated after nearly a whole day's dig and seeing their quarry get away, some of them pretty legless, and most not knowing a badger could swim.

Hit and Run Raids

The Germans continued their hit and run tactics. A friend of mine was harnessing a horse to a cart in a farmyard close to Kingsbridge. The routine was always the same. The horse was backed in between the shafts taking care that it did not step on a shaft thus breaking it, because some horses were clumsy and weighed over a ton. The shafts were lifted up and a rest stick was let down from underneath a shaft to hold the cart in place as the horse was attached. There were two tug chains, two breeching chains and a back chain to fix before pulling up the rest stick. The tug chains were fixed first, then the back chain leaving the breeching chains until last. He had attached one tug chain and was about to fix the other when a bomb fell on an empty building close by. The horse bolted with the cart, which was overrunning because no breech chain or back chain was in place. The cart was hitting the horse up the backside and the rest stick was hitting its legs. All my friend could do was hare around shutting all the gates and doors to prevent the horse escaping from the yard, injuring itself and smashing up the cart.

The Bombing of Aveton Gifford

In my case I was ploughing with an old horse (Prince) and a young one (Royal) on the day our village was bombed. I had heard the planes coming and gone to the horse's heads to calm them.[5] As soon as the bombs started to fall the young horse took fright and upset the older one. I did what I had been told to do, catch hold of one ear, lifting my feet off the ground so as not to be dragged under the horses and plough. With my other hand I pinched the horse's nose above the nostrils to cut off its breath and bring its head down. I did not think about running for cover, my job was to prevent the horses injuring themselves. In the event the only thing damaged was a broken rein which had twisted around the plough wheel on our two hundred yard dash across the field. The horses stood relatively calmly beside the hedge until the raid was over, I have often wondered if they knew they were safer there. The horses were always nervous after that when they heard a low flying plane, and so was I, looking up to see if there were black crosses on the wings, and heaving a sigh of relief when the RAF roundel showed up clearly. Farmers near the South Brent to Kingsbridge railway line were nervous too. If a German plane couldn't find a train to shoot up quickly it would fire at anything before scuttling back to France. We often laugh about our experiences now, but it was a fact of life then, and at times very frightening.

---

[5] On 26 January 1943 the 13th century Church took a direct hit as did the Rectory, and both buildings were destroyed. A little girl Sonia Weeks, aged five, a Plymouth evacuee staying at the Rectory was killed. David was one of the four teenage pallbearers at Sonia's funeral. There was severe damage to many of the village houses. David describes the scene in the village in his postscript. (See page 124.)

St Andrews Church pre World War 2.

St. Andrews - bombed by the German Luftwaffe 26th January 1943

Kingbridge Market, Ropewalk 1942.

Red Cross Sales at Kingsbridge Market

During the whole of the war Red Cross sales of live and deadstock were held in Kingsbridge market two or three times a year. A farmer was told to bring something for sale and to buy something to take home. It was in the auctioneer's discretion how many times an item would be knocked down before it was sold. A small item such as a hayknife may have been sold three times before a buyer was allowed to keep it; every 'buyer' was expected to hand over the purchase price whether he kept the item or not. All proceeds went to the parcels for prisoners of war fund. My father also went around collecting from farms and I used to drive him in the pony and trap and usually got a warm reception. On one farm we had a hostile reception and he was harangued by the farmer's wife who did not open the iron grill door but made her intentions clear by pacing up and down, then stopping to glare through it. It was the closest a human being had come to a wild, snarling, animal I had yet seen. After the war I attended a farmers' meeting when the guest speaker was a repatriated prisoner of war. His skin was the colour and texture of a lime washed wall, his hair had come out in great round patches, and looked if he might have had ringworm. Thanking us for the money raised he told us quite frankly that but for the Red Cross parcels he and his fellow prisoners would have died. It was a most moving moment.

With Mother and Father c.1943

By the middle of 1943 the army had started to run down the searchlight site, and the World War I Lewis machine gun had been replaced with a twin barrelled Vickers after the air raid on the village. It could fire at a tremendous rate which one guard found out after the previous guard had left the safety catch off. They had to scrounge fifty rounds to replace the spent cartridges to hush it up, otherwise there would have been a court martial. He had only pressed the trigger for a couple of seconds, it was fortuitous the gun was mounted pointing in the air. The searchlights and generators were still there with a skeleton crew, but most of the soldiers were moved on, so we had to find alternative casual labour.

The Land Girls

We tried German POWs as workers but I cannot remember where the camp was. I know I felt sorry for the German officer being bawled at by a British sergeant because something was not to his liking. I cannot remember why I had to ask for labour in person either as we had a telephone. We did not get on with them too well, they were surly and quite expensive for the amount of work they did. Other farms had Italian POWs who were cheerful and good workers, but there were no Italians near us so we settled for the Women's Land Army.

Land Girls came in all sorts and sizes. If one had a gang for threshing they came with a gang leader. My first experience of Land Girls came when I was still at school when I used to take the tea out to the harvest field as soon as I had changed out of my school clothes. Mum used to get extra rations for feeding harvest workers, but tea was in short supply. I would carry a large kettle holding about two gallons of tea in one hand, a basket full of cups, pieces of cake, sandwiches, bread and cheese in the other. By the time I had crossed three fields I knew I was carrying it. We were saving hay, there were two, probably three girls sat down together a short distance from the men with empty cups held out for me to fill. Dutifully I poured the ladies first and as I poured out the tea to the last girl, she commented:

"Do you call this tea? I call it bl --- y `ot water."

Land Girls with their harvest

It was the first time I had heard a woman swear, it seemed to make such an unforgettable impression with a Birmingham accent and I also took it as an affront to my mother who struggled hard with rationing. I never said anything, but in future tried to add a bit of extra tea to the pot without mother seeing.

Threshing

I admired the girls at threshing time, it was a filthy job if the wind was in the wrong direction. Doust is a local name for the shells covering the grain on the stalk and is separated in the threshing process from the grain and blown out underneath the thresher. It had to be kept clear of the thresher, as if that became blocked it would come out with the grain at the back of the machine and have to be threshed again. It got in your eyes, up the nose, down the back of the neck and barley ails would work their way through trousers. Later dust blowers came along, but not until after the war.

Land girls threshing. Picture Courtesy of Stuart Antrobus

When I got older and more authoritative I would make sure the girls were rotated, except for pitching sheaves to the feeder at the top of the machine. They always tried to get this job because it was up in clean air, but unless they were very strong they would slow down the whole operation, I always picked two strong men for that job to keep up a steady pace the whole day. There would be two men on the machine, one feeding the threshing drum and one cutting the twine around the sheaves, two pitching to them, two on the straw rick, one pitching to them, one on the doust, two men bagging and stacking the grain sacks, and probably two wagons carting away the sacks. A team of twelve had to be kept busy.

Pasties

Each neighbour would lend a man or come himself to help and we would help them in return when they were threshing. Dinner was always provided by the farmer, and normally a dozen or so pasties would be ordered from the baker in the village. They were beautiful pasties, meat one end, potatoes and carrots the other, a large wholesome meal attractively presented in a large wicker basket. They never varied in quality despite the difficulties of getting the ingredients. A man used to come around with the threshing machine with the nickname of Pasty. It was said he once propped open a heavy five bar gate with his pasty to let the hunt through. The baker always made an extra large pasty and placed it on the top of his basket as a sort of trade mark. This pasty was supposed to be for the host farmer, but 'Pasty' would always get to the basket first to grab the large one despite efforts to hide it. One farmer whose ricks were next on the list went to the baker with a proposition; was it possible to blow up an empty pasty with a bicycle pump. Although the reader will think this story is a figment of my imagination, it is perfectly true and can still be verified. They spent the whole of a Sunday afternoon perfecting the ruse, and the result was a huge, perfectly browned empty pasty. The rest of the threshing team were forewarned to watch Pasty bite on thin air.

War Time Cereal Growing

Cereal growing was a bit of a hit and miss affair, it was before the advent of herbicides, or pesticides for that matter. We always tried to rotovate the crop of weeds before planting the crop but in our damp climate it was not always possible. After years of being down to grass, once it was ploughed every weed under the sun sprang up. Fields would be blood red with poppies, or bright yellow with charlock, sometimes black with thistles. If the infestation was too great and the crop looked like being badly affected we were not allowed to plough it up, and could be summoned to appear before the magistrates if we did. The crop had to be weeded by hand. It is a daunting task to be confronted with a large field full of charlock, and at the end of the day I used to feel quite sick from the smell of the flowers.

The Evacuation of Six Parishes

The whole of the coastline along the south coast of England was mined above the high water mark, and concrete pillars and anti tank obstacles covered every exit from the beaches to thwart the invasion everyone expected after the evacuation of Dunkirk. Rumours started to circulate thick and fast when sappers started blowing up the mines laid in Slapton Sands. Then the news came that almost the whole of six parishes[6] were to be evacuated, in all twenty five square miles, to make room for a live ammunition training area for the United States Forces. The inhabitants of those parishes were profoundly devastated. Those farms outside the area were asked to do what they could to accommodate livestock so that a nucleus would be available when those who were evacuated were able to return after the war. They were given six weeks to get out by Christmas 1943.

Emergency sales of stock in Kingsbridge market were held every two weeks, but prices were low because of the onset of winter. Winter food supplies did not exist for the extra stock to be absorbed outside of the area, so every contractor with a hay baler or threshing machine was ordered into the area to bale hay ricks and thresh the corn. I volunteered to help our contractor three days a week, the most my parents could spare me, to bale hay with a stationary baler using wire for trussing the bales. I was one of a team of seven, paid for by the Ministry of Agriculture, going from farm to farm. We became a tight knit hardworking team of friends, hardly ever seeing the farmer or being

---

[6]Blackawton, Chillington, East Allington, Sherford, Slapton, Stokenham, Strete and Torcross. There was to be a sudden total evacuation of these six parishes involving 3,000 people, their possessions, farm stock and equipment. The date fixed for completion of the evacuation was 20th December 1943. The Slapton Sands area and South Hams was chosen for training the United States Forces because it resembled the beaches in Normandy where they were to land on D-Day.

aware of the heartbreaking ordeal of those having to leave their homes. There were four Land Girls in the team who never missed a day through sickness; they just got on with the job of helping those poor unfortunate people who had to leave their farms, and they worked hard and unstintingly, dreaming of what they would get up to on the fortnight's leave to be awarded at the end.

The deadline of Christmas was extended to New Year's Eve. When darkness fell on that day we still had not finished the rick we were baling so the driver turned on the tractor lights to finish because of the obvious dangers of working with pulleys and belts. When we finished we embraced the girls, wished them luck, and I never saw them again.

The tractor, baler and the few hay bales left over had to be out of the area by midnight or it was rumoured we would be shot by the Yanks; we had already seen them armed to the teeth getting stuck in the lanes with their huge transporters. One of the team was an old man in my youthful eyes, and on our four mph journey to the edge of the area at Blackawton mentioned that he had never been on the road after midnight on New Year's Eve; he was very superstitious and worried he would be a lost soul wandering the lanes for evermore. The contractor's wife, knowing my parents would be anxious, turned up to take us both home. I got in the door on the stroke of midnight.

My Mentor gave up his farm, he and his wife went to live in a cottage, but he still helped us as well as other farmers. Still keen that I should use my eyes to save money he admonished me one day for buying a shovel stick:

"Couldn't 'ee see one growing in the 'edge?"

His farm was taken over by an evacuated farmer from Sherford.

CHAPTER 4

D Day

We were too far away from the battle training area to know what was going on in there. Two Typhoon fighter bombers flew low over us every morning at eight, so punctual you could set your watch by them, en route from the airstrip at Roborough to drop their bombs in the training area. A friend of mine living just outside the area told me they used their machine guns and cannon as well. I learnt later that a Typhoon's firepower could be as deadly as a light cruiser's broadside. I felt sorry for the American troops being bombed as part of their training, but felt it was in some way a payback for enticing away all the pretty girls with their gifts of nylon stockings. Farmers on the coastal farms west of Dartmouth had an unforgettable ringside view of the D Day rehearsals when on several occasions the whole of the sea from Dartmouth to Start Point would be filled with three hundred ships.

CARELESS TALK COSTS LIVES

The build up to D Day affected many of us, no one was allowed anywhere near a military convoy because security was so tight. If someone accidentally wandered into a restricted area they could be detained indefinitely, and their family would be told they were safe but under arrest. At times the main road would be blocked with military vehicles, and families would be shut up in their houses for hours on end, listening to the din outside of screaming engines in low gear, and the monotonous rattle of caterpillar tracks negotiating the tight corners. Fields bordering the main road were taken over by men and equipment under camouflage nets. The 'Careless Talk Costs Lives' and 'Be like Dad keep Mum' slogans we had lived with since the outbreak of war had their effect. We were too scared to talk to one another about anything we had seen in case we were divulging secrets which might be of assistance to the enemy and could land us in jail. Anyway we were all too keen that the invasion of Europe should be a success and the dreaded war ended to think otherwise.

Death of a Local Hero

When Alvar Liddell announced over the radio on 6th June 1944 that the invasion of Europe had begun we all felt as if a huge weight had been lifted off our shoulders, only to be burdened down with grief a few days later when a greatly respected young soldier, Sapper JWH Martin DCM, was buried in the churchyard. His parents farmed at Staunton. He had escaped from the rearguard action at Dunkirk, and by using his countryman's evasive and foraging skills had tramped all the way through France and Spain to Gibraltar, returning to England four months later. He volunteered to be in the first wave to land on the Normandy beaches and died of the wounds received in the attack. It seemed that the whole of the parish together with representatives from every organisation in the district attended the laying to rest of one of their sons. Six tall guardsmen carried him to the grave and fired six shots each, startling into flight scores of pigeons resting in the nearby trees. Our bombed out church kept watch poignantly over the proceedings.

Farms contracted to the American Forces to supply milk and fresh produce were badly disrupted by their sudden departure, yet it proved quite easy for them to switch their supplies on to the home market. Not so lucky was a farm contracted to take all their waste food in the form of swill. Things were going along very nicely until the G.I.s left, then suddenly there were hundreds of pigs to feed with nothing to feed them on.

Catching Fleas

Very soon after D Day our workman accidentally cut his hand with a hook, completely severing the tendon to his forefinger, and so would be off sick for months. Then we had a live-in Land Girl who sparked off Dad's fear of fleas, and because she had an American sailor boy friend he reckoned she was bringing fleas home. It was true he caught a flea. One evening he called for me to come to the bathroom where he was standing naked in the bath having shaken his clothes out, and pointing to the insect barely visible against the white porcelain he wanted me to catch it. I recalled My Mentor at Waterhead telling me the way to catch a flea in the bed. You had to lick two fingers and estimate where the flea would jump before carefully placing the two fingers on the miscreant; from what I recall, a flea always hesitates before the next jump. Anyway I managed to despatch the flea much to Dad's relief. Afterwards I asked him why he had put the plug in:

"So as to make sure it did not go down the plug hole without my seeing it," he said, *"otherwise I would still itch."*

Afterwards I wondered why having seen it he had not washed it down the plug hole. Fleas never bothered me as I could catch scores from picking poultry, while mother went running for the nicotine bottle as soon as she saw one.

The Land Girl was a Eurasian from Liverpool and extremely conscientious, well trained and good with cows, spotless in the dairy, and I was pretty sure she was not the originator of the flea. She was not with us long before catching cow pox and going off sick. I suppose having started milking early in small doses I was immune.

A New Land Girl

The WLA supervisor brought another girl who had been evacuated from Slapton when the Americans took over the farm she worked on. She then worked as a relief on a farm near Salcombe during the run up to D Day, milking, and delivering the milk in the town. The town was full of Americans keeping fit by running up and down the hills in columns of threes. Never so disciplined as our boys they would call out to her when she was making deliveries, expecting a smile and a wave as they ran by. When they left on 6th June the town was so silent to be almost ghostly. She was due to start on another farm in September but in the meantime could help us out.

Sheila, soon to be Mrs Balkwill, in her land girl uniform

She too was good with cows, good tempered, very hard working, had a soft Welsh intonation with a spot of Irish picked up from her grandmother, and a delightful smile. We were very busy with acres of corn to cut and stook. I had been urging Dad to keep more cows as the WAEC looked favourably on them and would accept a lower acreage of potatoes; I did not like spuds and had increased the cows to eighteen. She never minded the long hours, even when I told her my parents were reluctant to pay overtime, telling me she had never been paid overtime and was quite happy to take a day off when it was raining to do any necessary shopping. During her stay she had convinced me that my duty was towards my elderly parents, and not to join the army for revenge. Then it was time for her to move on to the next farm three miles away.

During August we had a boys' school from near the water's edge at Devonport housed in the big barn. On the whole they were good workers, going from farm to farm harvesting corn and picking up potatoes. At first the masters banned them from swimming in the river, but it was like trying to keep ducks out of water on the full tide and in the end the masters relented and organised water events. The only complaint I heard of their presence was from Lekatere who was semi-retired and lived on the bridge. One night all his apples suddenly went missing from his orchard.

A Slaughterman's Licence & My First Car

I was then seventeen, and having been initiated into the art of killing a pig was suddenly confronted with an edict that those who killed pigs must have a slaughterman's licence issued by the local authority. I duly presented myself to an official in a dingy office of Kingsbridge Rural District Council, now the depot for dustbin lorries. I suppose I must have answered correctly all of the questions asked because I came out a fully fledged slaughterman. I was old enough to drive a car. After a few lessons my parents considered I was fit to drive and bought a second hand Standard Nine. Mother had got fed up travelling on the bus with her shopping and Dad condescended to let me drive him to market, shouting hoarse commands when approaching vehicles had to be avoided. So I combined the two jobs and was allowed the use of the car to go to a dance. I did not have to pass a driving test because they were suspended for the duration of the war. This is a fact never forgotten by any of my offspring when they had passed their tests!

Strangely enough Dad had consented to me taking dancing lessons in the village when I was fifteen. Although he had an abject fear I would be seduced by some pretty maiden he thought dancing would cure my flat feet, a complaint I did not have, but one he thought I should have inherited from him. I had to make the necessary arrangements to pick up a spare part from the machinery engineer to legalise the use of petrol for anything other than market. The police were very hot on the misuse of petrol, and I was stopped on several occasions until de-rationing. A friend trained a young boar to hop in and out of a trailer whenever he wanted to go to a non-agricultural event, and was not stopped once. Farms situated in walking distance of a beach or dance hall became popular places to leave one's car.

A Tractor Arrives

A tractor had also been ordered for when I was seventeen, but unknown to us until we ordered it, there was a twelve months' waiting list. To add to the frustration, because the Japanese controlled most of the world's rubber plantations we could only have a tractor with iron wheels, so it could not be driven on the road in any case.

This was a period in agriculture of innovation and adaptability in the change-over from horse to tractor. We must have bought a tractor-drawn plough at the time, but used horse implements to work the ground down for quite a while. I remember taking off the shafts on the wagon and fitting a drawbar for the tractor, likewise fitting a drawbar to our neighbour's horse-drawn binder and cutting his corn as well as ours.

A 1940's iron wheeled Fordson Tractor

If a farm had a two furrowed plough they continued to use it, the tractor driver getting off at each end to turn the plough over, or if he was lucky, getting his father to ride on the plough to do the turning. True it was faster than the three horses pulling it would be, but it took an extra man. In the end one had to have tractor machinery for tractors, which within twenty years was to change again when the three point linkage system was invented, and all machinery was mounted on the tractor instead of trailed. Old lorries were much sought after to make trailers, and the axles were cut and a flat bed fixed on the axle, with lades and sides added to the bed. These can easily be spotted in old photographs by the original transmission housing on the axle. We were encouraged to become mechanised with the veiled threat that soldiers returning from the war would not work antiquated machinery, but it was some time after the war ended before the soldiers returned, staying on to help the countries occupied by the Germans back to democratic civilian rule, and to counteract the Russian threat to peace.

CHAPTER 5

Post War

The war in Europe ended in May 1945, but there were still the Japanese to beat, although in comparison to Europe they seemed far enough away. With the euphoria there was time to reflect on the incredible feats of courage, devotion to duty and help for one another by civilians and service people throughout the war. A returning soldier told me that during the Battle of EL Alamain, which incidentally lasted twelve days, an extraordinary length of time for any battle, he was twenty miles behind the German lines when he came across two little old ladies serving tea and biscuits from a Salvation Army van in a wadi. When he asked them how on earth they had managed to get there, they shrugged off his concern saying:

'We thought we would be needed."

This and many similar stories summed up the spirit which got us through the war.

By this time I had been captivated by the pretty Land Girl with the soft Celtic accent. She had returned just before the war ended to work with her original employer at Slapton to find an airstrip had been bulldozed right through the level area of the farm. The farmer was depressed and in conflict with the War Damage Commission, and the cows were slow in returning so all she did day after day was pick up stones which were scattered across the fields from the bulldozed hedges. The fun fair returned to Kingsbridge in late July for the first time since the outbreak of war. It should have been an evening of jollification for us but the crowds jostling in the small area in the Kingsbridge Recreation Park were suffocating. The dodgems started off at sixpence (2½p) a ride and because of the demand went up in stages to two shillings (10p) before the night was out. I was earning less than £2 a week at the time. I wanted to impress her with my shooting, but either the airguns were fixed or the crowd knocked me off balance and I did not shoot down enough cats to win her a prize.

Portrait of David sent to Sheila as a keepsake 1945

She then told me she had decided to resume her interrupted nursing career in London. She wanted some qualification for her life ahead and could not see any future working on farms: as far as the WLA was concerned she had done her bit and was free to leave. I was ready for a commitment although I was far too young with virtually no prospects. She was not so sure, we were of different religious denominations, almost an impossible barrier in those days. She needed time to think properly and to readjust. To me London was the other side of the world. If one takes into consideration the number of young farmers who eventually married ex-Land Girls there must have been countless young men in a similar situation to me at that time.

Young Farmers

Life went on. There seemed to be more restrictions rather than less. I had joined the Young Farmers Club (YFC) as soon as I had transport. The clubs were ridiculed in some circles as a dating agency, but I found a seat of learning and competition. We were addressed by successful farmers and were able to visit their farms. We were taught by top class instructors to select dairy stock, breed sheep for the future meat trade, and select beef cattle. We learned to strip down and service tractors. All the things that a modern agricultural place of learning does today which we had been denied because of war's aftermath.

Sheep Shearing & Wool

My Mentor had taught me to shear so I entered YFC shearing competitions and was lucky enough to win a few. Wool had fetched good prices during the war when it was requisitioned by the Government. One of the aspects of shearing competitions was the care of wool when shearing, and its storage after. My father had instilled this into me from the time I had my first few ewes, particularly in keeping grass and bits of string away from the fleeces. He never used artificial colourings, always saying what was the point in dyeing wool red when the natural colour of our Devon soil was that colour anyway. Wool experts graded the wool on the farms then, a highly skilled job because wool has about a hundred different grades, from the very fine downland breeds to the very coarse almost hair like strands of the Scottish mountain breeds. Nowadays wool is all transported to the wool factories where it is graded in the best possible conditions.

Wool is not that easy to store. Sometimes during the war they did not come to grade it until the spring and so it had to be covered to prevent it becoming contaminated with hay and straw, and one year rats got into the pile. It was a haven for the rodents because it was dry and warm, ideal conditions for them to breed. We had to move the lot and try to catch the rats as they escaped. The Ministry paid a penny a rat's tail to encourage farmer's to catch them up, but it was never worth bothering with a small number. One year the threshing contractor cut off the tails of the rats caught at the bottom of the corn ricks on every farm. I suppose it would amount to several hundred in a season but I don't know who counted them. There was a rather haughty secretary in the WAEC office in Kingsbridge and I hoped he was going to tip them out on her desk for counting. Warfarin was not in general use then for killing rats and mice, and rat catchers had a concoction of poisons to use which was also very palatable to dogs. If you valued your dogs you didn't employ rat catchers but kept a couple of terriers.

As well as keeping extraneous rubbish out of the wool and avoiding excess raddle marking, it had to be kept dry, which meant the sheep were kept indoors if it was raining so as to be dry enough for shearing, or if there was a heavy dew shearing was delayed until the sheep were dry, especially in their breasts which is the last place to dry out. Having been taught all this I was flabbergasted to read that Durham farmers of old would shear their sheep and if the wool price was too low would bury it for a year or more. The writer reckoned it never rotted. I would have to see how they buried it to be convinced because every time ours got wet in store, the strands stuck together, turned a horrible yellow and was useless for cloth. He went on to say in Victorian times when the main east coast railway was built across the Cleveland bog they packed tons of wool into the bog and ran the rails over the wool, also in medieval times they packed wool into the river bed first before laying the bridge foundations. I can understand them doing that but never heard of it in the West Country. When they built the road across the Torcross Line they used faggots pressed into the shingle for the base. .

Still, the more uses which could be found for wool the better it would be for shepherds. We were told then that wool would never be under threat from man-made fibres because wool has a hollow centre in each strand which is absolutely ideal for insulation, one feature man could never copy. But these days the fashion conscious don't seem to need insulation, and in their centrally heated homes and offices, seem to delight in exposing their skin. Add the trend for carpetless floors and the result is disastrous for the wool industry.

I must mention here a fourteen year old girl who went to work on the looms at South Efford. Not only did she learn to spin and weave but how to dye the wool as well. As it was a trade secret she had to sign a document forbidding her ever to disclose any of the formulae. In later years she worked for us, I was interested to learn the concoction of natural dyes she used and pressed her hard to disclose them. All I ever got out of her was that they used the bath to soak the yarn in dye. I should have asked her whether they had another for the usual things one does in a bath. But to her eternal credit although the family had ceased to do any dyeing or weaving many years before, she refused to disclose any detail because she had signed this document and eventually the secrets died with her. It is good to remember and look back on such integrity.

Out of the blue came the threat of the 1947 Agriculture Act when tenant farmers would have security of tenure. I was young, ambitious and there was a large acreage across the road farmed by a tenant who could be there forever. There also was a large house which could be divided to accommodate two families, Sheila, the girl I adored, was recovering from a serious illness, she had decided to join my church and wanted to come back to Devon. My parents gave the tenant notice to quit at Lady Day 1948.

(Lady Day was a traditional day on which year-long contracts between landowners and tenant farmers would begin and end in England and nearby lands. Farmers' time of "entry" into new farms and onto new fields was often this day, and as a result, farming families who were changing farms would travel from the old farm to the new one on Lady Day).

Winter 1947

Estate agents found it difficult to cope with the amount of work. Many of my friends were going into partnership with their parents and setting up home either in the farmhouse or in a cottage. But first we had to cope with the 1947 winter.

I had not experienced anything like it. Snowdrifts higher than the hedges, with sheep driven before the storm buried in them, cattle out in the field needing extra feeding, and the tractor frozen up and refusing to start. My little dog located all the sheep bar one fairly quickly, and even that one emerged from the melting snowdrifts ten days later thin but otherwise unharmed. We had to beg, borrow and steal milk churns for the accumulated milk which was eventually picked up from the main road still frozen. Turnips were frozen so hard the sheep could not eat them, and redwings and fieldfares migrating from Scandinavia were dying by the hundred. We used the horses for feeding the stock, their feet became so balled up with the snow we had to scrape them out every ten minutes. But it could have been worse, more than a million sheep in England and Wales perished that winter.

Return to Court Barton & Marriage

On Lady Day 1948 we moved back into Court Barton, moving my parents' furniture by horse and wagon. Sheila and I had a kitchen table and a bed, I knocked up some orange boxes for bedside tables, whilst she scrounged coupons for curtains to cover them and the windows. We had used up all our allocation on the wedding. People were so kind, even the bank clerks in Kingsbridge were saving for us. My Mentor gave Sheila a rolling pin made from a piece of alder he had cut from beside the brook at Waterhead several years before, it was light, beautifully crafted and smooth from hours of sandpapering. There was the usual comment of keeping me in order as well as what it was designed for. Secretly I thought it would not last long because it was made from soft wood and would easily be dented. How wrong I was. It is still with us after over fifty years, still perfectly smooth and round, with only one small chip on the end where Sheila dropped it on the stone floor of the kitchen at Court. He was incredible in his knowledge of country skills, that piece of wood must have been perfectly seasoned.

David's Wedding at Emmanuel Church, Plymouth 31st January 1948
(Aveton Gifford church was still in ruins)

L to R - Grandfather Jago, Henry Balkwill, Dorothy Balkwill, cousin David Balkwill best man, David and Sheila, Molly Balkwill, Sheila`s aunt and uncle Mr and Mrs Rees.

I was anxious to increase the cows and had eight in-calf heifers ready to calve in the Autumn, I also wanted to become tuberculin tested as the milk was worth quite a bit more. Out of the eight in-calf heifers, seven reacted. It was a bitter blow. We did not have enough stock to utilise the extra grass acreage so we put nearly sixty acres in the spring grass sale. It would be a heavy work load looking after all that stock; in the event it made good money but the buyers overstocked to get their money back which caused even more work to keep the stock in. It was a dry summer after the awful winter, the cereals did well and on the last barley field we had a contractor to combine the crop. This was the first combine harvester to be seen in the parish with almost the whole village coming up to watch. We already had more straw than we needed, the price of straw was not covering the cost of baling so I burnt it.

Sheila and David's Father Henry Balkwill with the Standard 9

One farmer thought I had committed a heinous crime saying that if he had known I was going to burn it he would have picked it up himself. It was a practice which was to become quite common because it burnt the weed seeds and provided a wonderful seed bed for the next crop. One of the bonuses of the 1947 winter was a fantastic crop of butterflies. We had a pear tree in the orchard which was almost inedible because it was for making perry. When the pears dropped and started to rot the ground was covered with masses of drunk butterflies of every description. We had a Polish farm student at the time whose hobby was studying them and he had a field day.

Goodbye to the Horses

There soon came a time when we had to say goodbye to the horses as tractors had superseded them. They became stiff from inactivity, were eating their heads off and prone to laminitis. Nobody wanted them for working but there was a great demand for horses on the continent. I tried to forget they might land up on someone's table, and when I could not, would console myself that the Belgians were starving. When I took the dealer to see them and told him the price, I knew immediately by his quick acceptance that I had not asked enough. Ever after for a private sale I haggled, to the end those horses were teaching me a lesson.

One of the downsides to the war was the practice of paying building contractors cost plus ten per cent by the Ministry of Works. In other words they would get ten per cent above the cost of labour and materials. This negative outlook would persist for a very long time after the war, and there was also a restriction of ten pounds for any new work. I wanted a drain laid across the lower yard so we could lay down stone and rubble from the bombed church. I had dug the trench myself and bought old gas pipes from the scrap metal merchant; all I wanted was a gulley to catch the water from the roof and cowshed with an inspection chamber half way along the pipe. But when the builder told me it had come to more than the ten pounds authorised I was taken aback and decided to learn building work as I went along. I had a pretty straight eye from when I was taught stone walling. I wanted to put in a milking parlour to machine milk, to separate TB reactors from the rest of the herd, and to tear out all the old wooden stalls to prevent the cows breathing on one another and passing on the infection. In the end it was all accomplished and we became tuberculosis free.

Telephone Installed .... Baby Expected!

Mother had a telephone installed soon after we moved back to Court Barton. The telephone exchange was at Loddiswell and operated mostly by a woman but sometimes one did hear a male voice. The woman had a reputation for listening in to conversations, and as the telephone was a relatively new device anyone listening to a private natter between housewives was considered evil. Sheila was expecting our first baby and there were complications, the baby was large and riding high, which put pressure on her heart and gave her tachycardia. One evening she turned blue and I called the doctor out urgently, after that we were seeking constant advice by phone from her medical carers. Late one Saturday afternoon I met a GPO linesman up Chantry road looking for our house. This was most unusual because the country was on a five day week and I thought only farmers had to work weekends. In explanation he said:

"The old lady at Loddiswell said I must be sure to repair your telephone before I left work because there was a baby expected in the house."

We did not even know the phone was out of order as we had not tried to make any outgoing calls that day. "Th' oll woman" on the line at Loddiswell might have been the devil incarnate to some, but to me she was a guardian angel.

Village Entertainment

Village entertainment had continued throughout the war with a monthly travelling film show during the winter, and the very occasional touring professional entertainment party imitating the Crazy Gang, Tommy Handley, etc, with local singers, contortionists and conjurers for good measure. The Women's Institute were always looking for someone with a zest for making a fool of themselves at their annual party. Sheila and I became involved in amateur dramatics. The village was lucky to have a retired Shakespearian actor resident in the parish and willing to put a little polish on the proceedings. It was not easy, one of the shopkeepers was very keen but with the unfortunate habit of forgetting her lines. We would be doing a scene, then all of a sudden she would get a bout of amnesia and leave the stage with an excuse like having to put the kettle on or something similar which would leave the rest of the cast staring at each other open-mouthed. She was too deaf to hear the prompter and too useful in the supply of refreshments to be sacked, the rest of the cast had to learn her lines as well as their own so she could lip-read and remain on stage. We used to do all sorts of plays from Shakespeare to country pieces, always changing the name to avoid royalties. Sheila's piercing scream when she was about to be murdered would make even my hair stand up on end. A set of Welsh plays were popular because they translated into Devon dialect very well. We did a play called The Poacher once, our tutor had accurately dressed me for the leading role. As I walked on stage a wag in the front row called out:

"David you look just like Noah Parsons."

This remark brought the house down, making it very difficult to keep a serious face or instil any gravity into the play. Alas the arrival of television killed village plays stone dead. No one would pay to watch amateur efforts when they could witness first class acting on the box.

Village life began to pick up the shreds of pre-war sporting activities. A football team was started up, there were Royal Marines still stationed at the Thurlestone Hotel, and we played a team from there one Saturday afternoon. They very quickly made it twelve-nil in the first half, but deemed it superstitiously wrong to score any more goals and for the rest of the match they had us running around in circles trying to get the ball from them. But Aveton Gifford could never beat Thurlestone village or Loddiswell at football. There was a cricket club before the war and when it was revived in the early fifties it thrived, mainly by the enthusiasm of Reg Moore. He was a very useful left arm fast bowler and could put together runs when needed. He had the right philosophy for cricket.

"If you are lucky enough when bowling to hit a batsman in his most tender spot, when he is doubled up with pain, go up to him, pat him on the back, shake his hand and say how sorry you are. Then from a longer run try to hit him in the same place again."

The motor car killed the village team in the end as when a cricketing family acquired a car the wife wanted the husband to take the family shopping or to the beach rather than watch cricket. I suppose things may be different now where there are two cars to a household.

Food Rationing

Food was still in short supply. I remember going to a meeting and being told by the speaker that young farmers had had the worst education possible with five years of rising prices. We did not believe him at the time but he was right. Food rationing ended in 1954 and the Ministry of Food stopped buying all the animals sent for slaughter. We were thrown on to the open market which was quite a shock as previously the Ministry would buy anything, and now we had to select our market which was quickly becoming quality orientated. We were also overrun with rabbits and I did not know what to do. I had been on a farm which allowed free rabbiting, the farmer certainly had them under control and said to us if we did not get rid of the rabbits they would get rid of us, but when I put forward this proposition to my father he would have none of it. He was appalled at the thought of every Tom, Dick and Harry sprawling over the farm with ferrets and guns, preferring to bring in a trapper, a relic I suppose of the depression in the early thirties when it was just as profitable to farm rabbits. The trapper also paid in cash, always an attraction to Dad.

The Rabbit Catcher

The rabbit catcher had a donkey, a sweet little thing which seemed able to carry twice her own weight. She was never more than two paces from him when she was working, either carrying dead rabbits early in the morning in the two panniers on either side of her back, or gin traps later in the day if he was laying them down.

Donkey with panniers typical of the area

In between times she would be let loose in a field and whenever she saw me she would gallop towards me with her long ears flapping. I could almost hear her purr as I stroked their silky skin. I discovered the trapper was leaving breeders, in other words he would leave a deep sunny hedge untrapped, preferably running north to south, and here the does bred early in the spring thus infesting the farm again before the following winter. Along with many farmers I bulldozed these cross hedges out to get rid of the rabbits, thus making larger fields for the inevitable bigger machines being invented, plus the fact we were getting a grant for doing it.

Rabbit hunters with their catch - 9 lads, 2 dogs and a flagon of cider. 1930

Aerial view of Court Barton circa 1955

Myxomatosis was reputedly first seen on a Kent farm where the tenant was in dispute with his landlord over ground game, (I believe that is a term for rabbits and hares.) I know no more than that, other than the fact it spread like a forest fire to the West Country because the rabbits had no resistance whatever, aided no doubt by well meaning farmers with a huge rabbit problem. I did not spread it, but was glad when it came then absolutely horrified to see what it did to the rabbits. I had always enjoyed rabbit whichever way it was cooked, especially a young rabbit at harvest time roasted in milk, but since the disease hit the rabbit population if I have eaten rabbit I have not enjoyed it. Since then we have not had a rabbit problem, as the numbers build up from time to time but the 'myxy' always seems to return to bring the numbers down again.

We continued with free range poultry for a while but foxes became an increasing menace. One night a fox got into a house and killed forty hens, biting the heads off most of them. One hen will feed a fox for four days. A poultry keeper would accept that sort of loss but a fox is a vicious killer of poultry and young lambs, so numbers have to be controlled with whatever means. We turned two large barns into deep litter houses. I had no liking for battery cages but in the end deep litter could not compete with the battery hen.

Left to right - Cousin Ben, Margie, Richard, Jenny, David & Sheila. July 1960

It must have been at the beginning of 1956. We had three children by then. I was coming home from Kingsbridge with all three when I came upon a flock of sheep being driven along the road between Offields Cross and Stadbury. I wound down the window and chatted to the drover. He was a partner in an enterprise to keep the grass down on Thurlestone Golf Course. Somehow the Club had managed to prevent the course from being ploughed up during the war, much to the disgust of the farmers around who were burdened with their various quotas. I presume people still played golf despite the sheep mess on the greens. He was moving the sheep to winter quarters farther along the road. He was a bit lame and a few of the sheep at the back of the flock were even lamer, so progress was slow, I was in no hurry, and no car came up behind me. I was just content to talk about sheep and try to learn a little from a vastly experienced shepherd. John and Margi were in the back all agog, and Richard still a baby was on the front seat beside me in a carry cot. We seemed to have so much more time in those days to enjoy conversation. When he reached the destination gateway for his flock he leant through the window and surveyed the children and spoke almost to himself:

"Two in the back and one in the casket. Young man, you'm spending too much time in 'ome."

Farm Students

We had several farm students down through the years starting with an ex-RAF Flying Officer fighter pilot. He had inherited a large fortune and was using the repatriation scheme to learn farming. He went on to buy a three hundred acre farm in Gloucestershire with a herd of a hundred Ayrshires. Was I envious? Then came the Pole. Winston Churchill had promised the Polish Brigade if they succeeded in ousting the Germans from Monte Casino in Italy they would be retrained and given jobs in this country in whatever they wanted to do. The chap whom we had trained first as a jeweller, then took up training in agriculture but this did not suit him either, so he then went into the hotel trade, all at the expense of the British taxpayer. The most satisfaction we had was with a mentally retarded lad. Somehow he seemed to have an affinity with animals, and I wished we could have had more like him. He was the son of an airman and born a 'blue baby' on an isolated station abroad, and did not get his blood changed quickly enough. When he left us he joined the army and was deemed expert enough to drive a tank. Then we took on a lad who turned out to be a schizophrenic; one day he would be fine, the next awful. He ended up by ramming buckrake toes (tines) through two tractor tyres at silage time. Sadly we had to end this work, machinery was just too expensive.

We employed a retired ex-dockyard worker to repair the stone pillars behind gateposts and to build concrete water troughs for the growing dairy herd. Cows congregate in gateways and love to rub their heads against a hedge. They always have and always will. Dad's stockman would say:

"They like to feel the earth piddling down over their faces."

It was even worse then because they had horns and would demolish a hedge in no time at all. It was possible to protect hedges with barbed wire but not in gateways, the cows could rip their sides as they jostled each other through.

Baccy

This old chap chewed tobacco, when he spat a stream of juice would shoot from his mouth upwards of three paces. I was talking to him down by the marsh one day, admiring the pillar he had just about finished when a stray dog from the village came along and cocked his leg against the handiwork. This to the builder was the ultimate humiliation. He spat at the dog and the stream of tobacco juice caught the dog in the eye. It must have stung because I can hear the dog now yelping all the way back to the village. On another occasion he was building a trough in a field and he noticed my dog sliding along the ground on her bottom, a sure sign of worms.

Your dug 'as got worms!" He remarked.

"I know." I said, *"I have tried several wormers and none seemed to have any effect."*

"Bring 'in over yer." He commanded.

I called the dog over, and meanwhile he had extricated a chew from under his hat band and was masticating away. After a few moments he extracted the chew from his mouth, and while I held the dog he placed the chew on the back of her tongue which she swallowed. I thought no more of it and continued talking about piping the water into the trough, but literally within what seemed like ten minutes I noticed the dog passing off a round rope of worms. On examination there must have been at least twenty tape worms about a foot in length. Replying to my incredulity he remarked:

"The same would 'appen to you if you chewed baccy."

They said he was a communist so I avoided discussing politics with him. The Pilot Officer was about to take part in the victory parade in London, or over it in his case. Just before the parade I sent him to help the old man carry some concrete blocks. He came back to the house very angry and red in the face.

"Don't you ask me to work with that silly old sod again!"

Apparently the old man had been moaning the whole time about how much money the capitalists were going to make out of the victory parade.

Technical Progress

We had been using artificial insemination on the cows since the end of the war when Dartington Hall instigated a cattle breeding centre. It was a period of extraordinary technical progress. Plant breeders were turning out better varieties of seed almost on a conveyer belt system by selective breeding of different strains of grasses and cereals. Most varieties were capable of doubling yields by being shorter and stiffer in the straw, and thus able to withstand heavier applications of fertiliser without lodging. In animal husbandry too breeding was a precise science with the use of hormones and fertility treatment, but as usual university scientists went over the top by breeding an animal with five limbs, so evoking the term of 'mad scientist.' Better fungicides and pesticides came onto the market. One could hardly keep up mentally with the changing names of varieties; girls names were easy to remember, but when the plant breeding station at Aberystwyth went all chapelly and started using numbers, one had to rely on experts.

Henry Balkwill with the Dairy Herd 1966

Avon Farmers

By the mid 1960's farm profitability was getting increasingly precarious. After a meeting one evening several of us were moaning about the fact that our inputs were going up in price while our outputs were stable or going down, simply because we were such small units, and had no buying or selling clout. Then someone told us to stop moaning and do something about it. A farmer's group had already started up in Gloucestershire so a few of us went there to see how it worked.

Basically it was pooling all orders for feed, fertilisers and fuel, and going straight to the manufacturer thus cutting out the middleman. When news of this venture got out it caused a furore. There was already a farmers' co-operative in the area but we did not think it was doing a good enough job in keeping our costs under control. Likewise we decided to send our stock for slaughter direct to the abattoir rather than the market to cut out the dealers and the transport to the market. There were eight of us in the venture, and we were soon joined by a number of others to make it worthwhile. There was no doubt we put a floor in the market for the stock sold off the farms, and lowered the prices charged by the merchants as they cut their overheads to compete. However we did not have the success that farmer's co-operatives were having in France, so two of us went over to have a look. We quickly saw the reason. The co-operatives in France controlled the credit: if farmers required a loan they could only get it through a farmer's co-operative, and to get that loan they had to buy their requisites and sell their produce to the co-operative, whereas in this country farmers went to a bank for a loan.

Dairy Cows beside the River Avon 1966

We would never be able to get the support and control the French co-operatives enjoyed. British farmers are a proud breed of individuals who wish to control their own destiny, they want to be their own boss, and are deeply suspicious of co-operative operations.

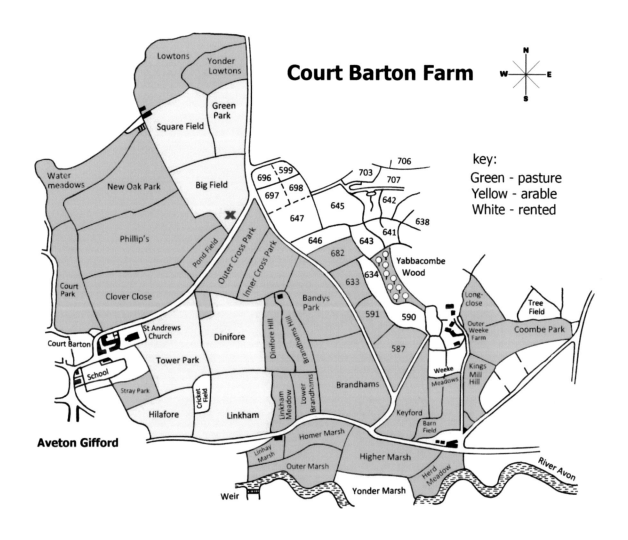

Map of Court Farm circa 1965

✖ *marks the spot where David was ploughing on the day of the bombing*

The buying side of the group fared better than the selling side and still continues, but not with the ideals of when we first started. The selling side of the operation depended on throughput, and the greater the volume the better the price we could get. I suppose twenty five percent of local farmers were utterly loyal to us. Fifty per cent used us, but would sell elsewhere if they could get a better price, some for as little as a farthing a pound (0.125p) and that was before decimalisation. The rest stuck to the gamble of the markets. There was a great demand for brucellosis free Friesian heifers for export to

Brittany. At first I was given the task of meeting the French buyers and escorting them around the farms to inspect these heifers because I could speak a little French. It was important to listen to their discussions to gauge how interested they were, but I found I could not understand a word they were saying, then realised they were speaking in Breton; they would talk to me in French but speak to each other in their own language. As the volume of business increased we employed an interpreter but she fared no better, and until then she had not known they had their own language. After nearly fifteen years we handed the business over to another co-operative.

Court Barton with Little Court in the background 1967

Changing Times, Hard Decisions

In the mid 1970's not only did we have a government which seemed not a bit interested in home agriculture, but inflation climbed to twenty seven per cent. I could not get a quote for a ton of feed or fertiliser except on the day it was delivered. It was almost impossible to run a business properly. Then about the time of decimalisation we had an invasion of millions of cabbage white butterflies from the continent. It was before maize became popular for winter feeding dairy cows, and kale was grown a lot for strip grazing. Caterpillars hatched almost overnight, and armies of these things were on the march from one field of kale to the next. It was possible to hear them munching away, and when they crossed the road to another field of kale it stopped the traffic. Farmers predicted that joining the European Community would have a similar effect as that invasion of hairy insects.

Henry Balkwill, Court Barton. 1967

We had moved into a time when world food shortages were replaced by considerable surpluses. Villages had changed too, and the number of workers connected to farms had greatly decreased to be replaced by factory workers, office commuters, and holiday homes, and changing the attitude of the inhabitants towards farm smells and practices. All our drains went under the village and we were continually getting complaints about smells, particularly when we were making silage. There was not the room between the yard and the school to put in a series of lagoons for settling ponds, so we had to make the decision to move the dairy unit to another part of the farm or to give up cows. Ironically the official standards for setting up a new unit were far more stringent than updating an old one, coupled with the fact that our private water supply would not rise to any other place on the road than to the existing buildings. The move would be too costly so we sold the cows and ploughed up the pastures for growing cereals.

The decision we had to make was one which confronted many farms. Herd sizes had increased enormously to pay for the increased costs of hygiene, refrigeration, machinery for dung handling, bigger buildings to house the extra animals, and for food storage. The old existing buildings were of no further use simply because modern machinery was too big to get in them for cleaning. Then came the decision of what to do with the old buildings, to let them become ruins, industrial units or houses? Most farmers settled for housing thus making rods for their own backs. Small farms within the villages, in some cases like Loddiswell as many as five, disappeared to become dwellings, with the land taken over by neighbouring farms. For other farm buildings deep in the countryside it was not so easy. Quite often there were two farms close to one another, having been built many centuries ago to share a stream or spring. There was the difficulty of getting planning permission, to be followed later by the harassment of town dwellers buying the houses. One farmer told me:

"My neighbour has sold his buildings for housing and one dwelling will be less than fifty yards from my silage pit, look what problems that will cause."

On another, the farmer had a mill for grinding grain for his cows which was never used after dark. But the newcomers objected to the noise, and to being woken at five in the morning by sheep calling for their lambs.

David's parents Henry & Dorothy Balkwill 1971

Back in the 1970's Sheila and I decided to sell cream teas during the summer months. We had to get my parents to agree as they still owned the house and lived in part of it, and we had to get planning permission as the farmhouse is a listed building. We turned one downstairs room into a tea room by taking out one of the existing windows and putting in glass doors, and we bought tables and chairs light enough to be carried outside in fine weather. The project was a success and we recouped the cost of the structural alterations and the purchase of the tables and chairs in the first year, the sort of return farming had never been able to manage. We continued this for several years, and started taking in bed and breakfast guests when both my parents died. Guesthouse accommodation on farms in this district was nothing new, farmer's wives had been doing this since the depression of the thirties. What was new was a farmer swapping a milking apron for a domestic apron, and I had to bear the brunt of quite serious leg pulling from my contemporaries.

In the mid eighties we handed this part of the business over to my son and daughter-in-law. They continued to make a success of it, turning over more rooms to en suite accommodation, and through the Devon Farms holiday organisation were able to use their experience to help other farming families provide year round accommodation of a standard which tourists have come to expect.

PRECIS OF F.T ARTICLE FROM AUGUST 16TH 1966

Pioneer of a Trading Group

David Balkwill 1966

David was featured in The Financial Times of August 16th 1966. The article was no. 5 in a series on Britain`s Farmers written by the agricultural correspondent John Cherrington. The series of articles looked at farming practice in relation to marketing, featuring "brilliant individualists" who had the ability to disregard farming conventions. The article looked at the voice of the farming community which was stronger when heard collectively through groups and co-operatives. In choosing David it was seen as an opportunity to feature "Devonshire, a county that might be called a veritable reservoir of tradition"!

The article gives us a short history of David`s farming career from the time of him taking over responsibility for the farm in 1949 at the age of 22, and goes on to give us clear information about the livestock and arable enterprise in 1966. In 1949 the farming practice at Court Barton was typical for the district, with South Devon cattle and Longwool sheep. The livestock required many acres of roots for winter feeding and a small area for corn in addition to the large areas of permanent pasture. The fields, many of which were small averaging three to four acres, were divided by high banks. The South Devon cattle were prized for their high butterfat milk which commanded a premium.

The South Devons were gradually replaced by Friesians, and the article states that the loss of the premium was more than compensated for by the increase in milk yield, and the Friesian calves were just as economical to rear! (It is a different story today with the high value of good beef calves.)

In 1966 the long wooled sheep had been replaced by a winter flock of fattening sheep, following the cattle over grass and kale. There is mention of pigs being kept outside in the fields, with the sows farrowing in tin arcs. It was recognised that this was a healthier option for the pigs rather than using the old buildings in the yard. Fields were progressively enlarged, and most of the dry level land was put into an arable rotation. By 1966 the holding was 400 acres, which included 150 acres of steep land: there were 210 acres of barley, 100 milking cows and 120 followers, 100 sows, 1,000 laying hens, 200 fattening turkeys and a pilot scheme for table rabbits!

The dairy cows were milked in two herds, one of which David milked himself. David was aware of business weakness of the average small farmer, and became one of the founder members of a local trading group `Avon Farmers`. After five years in 1966 the group had a turnover approaching £1.5m. This group was one of several set up as a reaction against what was considered to be unnecessarily high prices for many bought in feedstuffs etc. The result of the activity of these groups was a significant increase in price cutting.

David was more interested in reducing the fluctuations in prices for produce from the farms, but this proved difficult due to many variables including foreign competition. Avon Farmers found it difficult to establish fixed price contracts for finished products like lamb and beef. Weaned pigs were sent at fixed prices to fatteners in the Midlands, as were calves and other `store` stock.

It was seen that buyers valued a continuing supply of stock at fair prices, without having to consider market fluctuation, but some farmers found it difficult to resist the temptation of short term price rises to sell outside the group.

The article concluded with the view that farmers would be forced to spend more time on their farms doing their own work and having less time for market-going!

CHAPTER SIX

THE END OF THE CENTURY

As we enter the new century it is time to reflect on the past and plan for the future. In the last few years farming seems to have lurched from one crisis to another. Young farmers, as we did, try to set up groups to improve their profitability: one can only wish them better luck than we had.

The Media

Mass communication from the media does not help. There is something about appearing on television which can bring out misguided arrogance in the most insignificant scientist and minister of the crown. First we had an extremely ill-thought out statement from a junior minister about salmonella in eggs, so the public stopped buying and ten thousand egg producers were forced out of business. We had statements from scientists who ought to have known better on the BSE crisis, alarming the public and making ministers bring in controls which were not necessary in order to convince the housewife that they were doing something, although they had no idea how to tackle the problem in the first place. Now scientists have come up with a theory that BSE is an auto-immune disease triggered by a bacteria known as acinetobacter which cannot be transferred to humans except by injection, and now believe new variant CJD may have been caused by vaccines made from BSE infected animals. If this is the case there was never any likelihood of getting nvCJD from eating beef.

There is not enough unbiased government research into food, and too much biased research by multinational companies who will benefit enormously if government agrees with their findings, as in genetically modified crops. One only has to take as an example a report based on Swedish experiments just after the war when it was stated that eating margarine would cause less heart disease than butter. It took more than twenty years to prove that report erroneous. We now have to use an organophosphorous sheep dip to control sheep scab, a systemic substance that is proving more harmful to some operators than the arsenic we used before the war. I suppose the most significant change in agriculture has been from manpower to machine.

A Man could Plough One Acre a Day

When I started this discourse I talked of four men to one hundred acres, now it is one man to two hundred. A man could plough one acre a day and now it is nearer twenty in the same time, or forty if the driver works long enough because tractors, unlike horses, do not tire. Nor does the tractor driver have to walk the twenty miles behind his team so is capable of much longer hours. It took twelve men to thresh a rick of corn producing about five tons of grain in a day, and now one man with a large combine can do it in an hour. But also gone is the wonderful companionship, and the comradeship of working together, along with the gossip at meal times. In its stead are very long hours alone in an air conditioned tractor cab and its detrimental effect on family life.

Husbandry is no different now than it was then. Farmers still rotate the crops to avoid the build up of weeds and disease, and erosion is taken care of by ploughing against the slope, because tractors unlike horses can plough uphill. Fungicides and pesticides have become so expensive that farmers are very careful in their use. We have seen more acreages of late-harvested crops such as potatoes, maize, and linseed: if we have a wet November, this does precipitate erosion in the run-off from the fields, which in turn creates problems with the river authority.

Pressure Groups

We have far more problems from pressure groups which were almost non-existent when I started farming, the most significant being badger protection. Farmers are not allowed to control them in any way, yet there are far too many badgers around. As I described earlier the numbers were insignificant at the turn of the century, but now there are setts all over the place, and these are highly dangerous to tractor drivers when the tunnels run out under sloping fields; it does not take much to turn a tractor over and if the bottom wheel goes through the earth's crust into a badger tunnel it will. In my opinion badgers are the main predator of ground nesting birds such as the skylark, partridge, pheasant, plover, and with them the hedgehogs, snakes, toads, frogs and lizards. The biodiversity of our countryside is being destroyed by a creature that looks appealing on television but is seldom seen because it is nocturnal. Whether it will eventually be proved that badgers spread tuberculosis we will have to wait and see, but it is significant that the increase of tuberculosis in cattle is in exact proportion to the increase in the number of badgers. Dr Stanton in a paper suggests there should be no more than one main badger sett to a square kilometre, which equates almost exactly to the three setts of this parish in the 1920's.

Foxes

My son keeps free range hens to produce eggs for their visitors who are extremely complimentary about the flavour and colour when they are dished out on their plates. Yet how many of them connect the flavour of free range eggs to the hen's main predator the fox, and would deny us the right to control this pernicious killer. I wish the urban population would realise how finely balanced nature is. Allow one predator to gain ground and it throws the whole equilibrium of the countryside out of synchronisation.

Organic Food Production

Many farms in this district are turning over to organic food production, a costly procedure, for it takes about five years to qualify to get the status. We are encouraged by government to become organic as there is a demand for organic food at the moment, yet as soon as there is a downturn in the economy organic purchases are the first casualty. If the government insists that the growing of genetically modified crops is necessary, then cross pollination is inevitable no matter what precautions are taken, and becoming organic will be a waste of time and money. Can Europe resist the march of GM crops when the rest of the world has plunged straight in? In North America half the soya bean crop will be GM this harvest, and about a third of the eighty million acres of maize. GM crops are grown in Brazil, China, Mexico, Japan and South Africa.

A Living from a Farm of 20 Acres

In my youth it was possible to make a living from a farm of twenty to thirty acres, now they tell me it takes two hundred and fifty acres. I know farms are much more specialised than they were fifty years ago, but on a mixed farm then twelve cows were the norm, now one needs one hundred and fifty to break even. Wool reached a peak price during the Korean War when the Americans stockpiled it, but last year the wool price fell to an all time low: on our farm the price of a fleece only comes to half of what it costs to pay the shearer to remove it. We are paid in two instalments by the Wool Marketing Board; a flat rate when the wool is delivered, and the difference between the flat rate and the sale price it realises the next year. I heard of a Jacob flock owner who received two pence a fleece which would be paid over two years. Cider making has virtually disappeared except in specialist areas such as Somerset. On the farm tourist side will visitors want to come to a Devon forced to build an extra one hundred thousand or so houses?

David demonstrating herding geese with his sheepdog Gyp.
Church Fete circa 1989

During the last two years housewives have been marvellous in supporting British farmers. I hope they continue to insist that all imported food, even if it is processed in this country, is labelled with details of the country of origin. Farmers in this country have far stricter rules of hygiene and welfare of their animals than other producers anywhere else in the world. Unless other countries are forced to impose on their producers the same standards as are imposed on us we cannot survive, because the large retailers will ultimately buy from the cheapest source.

I do not want to end on a note of bitterness. Sheila and I have had a wonderful life in the countryside. We were fortunate to have had a roof over our heads and enough to eat, and we have brought up four marvellous children who are healthy, hard working and live close enough to be in daily contact. I have been privileged to have worked in this beautiful area and had twenty years work ahead of me just outside the back door, while others have hours of commuting to work and back with the added fear of unemployment.

Reminiscing

I admit to reminiscing about times gone by when doors could be left unlocked, when honesty in government was unquestionable, when the young had the time to look after the old, when newspapers presented facts not sensational stories. This is a sign of old age. I read with concern about proposed legislation to ban the hunting of wild animals with dogs: it is like taking a sledge hammer to crack a nut. I was never in favour of the coursing of hares with greyhounds as the hare has little chance of getting away, yet quite in favour of foxhunting as most foxes outwit a pack of hounds with ease and seem to enjoy doing it. I am afraid once foxhunting is banned so too will follow shooting, which is the most efficient means of controlling foxes, then rod fishing. We must never forget the beauty of the British countryside with its hedges, coverts and small woods was originally created and still is maintained by landowners for the purpose of hunting and shooting.

Agri-business

One reads statements by economists that food production is inefficient, and that one hundred thousand farmers will have to leave the land so that agri-businesses and multi-nationals can farm thousands of acres to produce food more cheaply. Yet I submit those organisations would treat the land as a truly expendable commodity, and would switch to something more profitable when the going gets tough and leave the land derelict - not like the true farmer who will survive by the skin of his teeth and still care for the land because he loves it. I just hope there will be enough young men and women with the courage and energy to take the risks needed to care for the land long after we who are old no longer walk the fields. I hope too that they will be able to watch one of the great sights of the countryside, which is a pack of hounds casting for scent on the other side of a valley to those lucky enough to watch; then to hear the lead hound cry out as it picks up the scent, followed by the rest of the pack giving tongue, with the huntsman's bugle-like commands drifting along on the wind.

A True Story

I would like to finish with a true story which I think typifies the time when I was growing up. The village grocer had been buying beautifully crafted, yellow, half-pound rolls of butter from a farmer's wife for several years. One morning he said indignantly:

"Mrs Jones! Did you know the butter I bought from you last week was short weight"

Mrs Jones could not hide her surprise.

'Well that's funny, I couldn't find my eight ounce weight, so I used a half pound packet of your sugar instead."

David & Trix June 2013

POSTSCRIPT

It is now twelve years since I completed the previous pages, and in fact I had forgotten I had as I did not keep a copy. A representative of the Parish Council asked if they could have it printed. I was surprised and very pleased. On reading it again I felt I should elaborate on the village of Aveton Gifford as I remembered it and perhaps be less reticent with surnames.

My Nanny

My nanny was a girl called Ethel Salter who lived with her widowed mother in a small cottage above the Fisherman's Rest which was called The Kings Arms then. As I said previously she was a long legged girl and impatient with my short steps, and pushed me everywhere in a baby carriage. I loved her dearly; she was a substitute for my mother who was extremely busy with several servants to organise, and we had at least two farm workers living in as we had no cottages attached to the farm. On top of domestic chores my mother supervised the making of dairy products, calf rearing, pig feeding, and had a large poultry flock. Butter, cream and eggs as well as dressed poultry were sold at the door, or taken into Kingsbridge once a week to the market. The lady who peered down at me and said "*can't ee walk*" was Mrs Corner who helped mother out at times and lived at Waterhead. I was told later by my mother that she was one of fourteen children, who wore no knickers until she went into domestic service at the age of thirteen. I don't know why! But that shocked me! Ethel had relations in Church Street, Kingsbridge, and she would take me on a bus to visit them on occasions. The family would make a great fuss of me. Bill Wonnacott the head of the house worked for the railway, and this proved useful in later years when I drove cattle from the market to the railway station on Kingsbridge Fair Days; he would remember me and give me preferential treatment.

We were Self Sufficient

The village was completely self-sufficient. It had not changed in 200 years. The records of the Quarter Sessions in Exeter describe an event in July 1738 when 49 named persons were charged (see Aveton Gifford, A Heritage). Each man had his trade listed: Shopkeeper, Apothecary, Victualler, Miller, Labourer, Blacksmith, Tiler, Weaver, Serge Weaver, Carpenter, Butcher, Master Shoemaker and Yeoman. In 1938 all those trades were active except perhaps the apothecary, which I am sure was substituted at times by the veterinary practitioner. The children when they left school at fourteen could read, write, add, subtract, divide and multiply. Well equipped to be employed. The apprenticeships started at fifteen years old, and my father would always take one school leaver for twelve months or until they became fifteen and could start an apprenticeship. One of my early memories is of looking out of my bedroom window and seeing Eddie Hurrell come flying out of their back door where Bakers Terrace is now, jumping over the school wall, and running up the meadow pulling his braces over his shoulders so as not to be late for work, while the old bull looked at him wondering what was going on and shaking his head.

The Bowling Club 1935. Henry Balkwill on right behind the Reverend EG Payne

There were organisations to look after all needs. The Rev Payne looked after souls and bowls. He was head of the bowling club, and his wife organised the Mothers Union. Mrs Bowden and later Miss Ellis organised the WI, and it was she who gave Bob Steer and me a £1 each at the First Aid exams. Mother would spend most of January collecting subscriptions for the Nursing Association, which were graded to the family's ability to pay i.e. 6 shillings (30p) for labourers, up to 15 shillings (75p) or £1 for tradesmen and farmers. Mrs Froude retired in 1939 but continued helping with confinements. Miss Lethbridge was a St John Ambulance nurse; a small neat woman, I can see her now, hurrying along the village street in her white starched apron and cap, striped skirt and black stockings, and carrying her medical bag. I do not think there ever was a doctor living in the village. They lived either in Kingsbridge or Modbury. The latter was the preferred choice before the advent of telephones simply because Harraton Hill was a great deal shorter if you had to run and get a doctor, and there was always a chance of getting a pull back up Stoliford Hill if the Doctor was in a good frame of mind.

With my tuition from the carters in my father's stable I had a good command of the dialect. Hearing a carter call a horse a *"crabbed old sod"* when he nipped the carters arm when backing him into a cart became easily transferable when the farmyard cock attacked my bare legs and left them bleeding. Ethel would censure me no doubt fearing blame from my mother for my bad language, but the war changed the language used, my nanny moved on, we moved to Little Court and the village welcomed evacuees from the London Blitz. One of them was a cartoonist from the Daily Mirror, ensconced in the Kings Arms. I suspect he got teased for his accent, but he retaliated by drawing all the regulars in his daily strip. Dr Billy Steer the vet became Dr Silly Beer, I cannot remember what the landlady of the pub became, but likewise all the rest of the regulars were incorporated. I thought it was humiliating, but far from it, they enjoyed their year or so of fame. Unfortunately it was far too left wing a paper for my father to buy, so I had to hear all about it on the school bus. When the ferocity of the bombing in London eased the cartoonist returned and the caricatures ceased. There were other dialects, notably the Northumberland Fusiliers based in the school after Dunkirk. We could not understand a word they said.

Changes in Farm Ownership

War also caused a few changes in ownership of farms, mainly by wealthy fathers trying to keep their sons out of the army. They had no knowledge of farming, so some employed an experienced farm worker as a "hyne", sort of one grade below a manager, or relied on the goodwill of other farmers for advice. One woman at Venn started keeping geese and had already quizzed my father about their welfare. She accosted him outside the Church door in February that year,

"Mr Balkwill I have seen a wedding, when can I expect an egg?"

I can see the perplexed look on the faces of other members of the congregation now. Another who had bought Chantry:

"How can you tell when a bullock has red water?"

"Oh it will be away from the herd and look sleepy!" said my father.

"They all look ruddy sleepy to me" retorted the questioner.

Later after the war ex service officers spent their gratuities on farms, but they did not last long.

The Girls who Visited the Camp

I mentioned the search light site earlier. Now the years have gone by I can elaborate on the girls who visited the camp. I don't think for a minute anything improper took place as there was no privacy, except perhaps in a guard room which had no wall on the east side and was wide open to the wind in winter. They just wanted male company which was reciprocated with relish. They were a pretty sight, perhaps their summer dresses showed too much leg, too many bare arms, and more than a glimpse of bosoms. I was fifteen, and Dad and I would run into them as we crossed the road from the farm buildings at the end of work. I admired their vivacity, and wished that I was older. They would call out "*Hullo Mr Balkwill!*" Dad would grunt in reply; he just did not approve.

My Brother's Last Leave

Rabbits were in fierce demand. On my brother's last leave we set off with ferrets and nets to catch a brace of rabbits for him to take back to his landlady. We tried all day in burrows around the farm where I thought they would be, but we did not see a rabbit, poachers had cleared them all. In September 1942 we learned he had been killed in action. I can still see my mother opening that dreaded telegram with shaking hands. She cried bitterly. I had not seen her cry before and I did not see her cry again.

Rationing

Now a word about rationing. The food ration for an adult in 1942 per week was 1 shilling and 2d (6p) worth of meat, 6oz sugar, 2oz butter, 4oz margarine, 4oz cheese, (if you were a worker engaged in heavy work you got double the cheese per week). 1 pint of milk per day and 3 eggs per month.

RATIONING

After World War II started in September 1939 the first commodity to be controlled was petrol, but food rationing was introduced quite soon after that. On 8 January 1940 , bacon, butter and sugar were rationed. This was followed by meat, tea, jam, biscuits, cheese, eggs, lard, milk and canned and dried fruit. Strict rationing inevitably created a black market. This was illegal, and buyers could be tricked with cheaper substitutes such as horsemeat instead of beef. Almost all controlled items were rationed by weight, but meat, exceptionally, was rationed by price. (All prices need to be considered in the values of the time: the buying power of one shilling was much more than its equivalent (5p) in modern British currency.)

Fresh vegetables and fruit were not rationed but supplies were limited. Some types of fruit which had been imported all but disappeared. Lemons and bananas became virtually unobtainable for most of the war; oranges continued to be sold but greengrocers customarily reserved them for children and pregnant women, who could prove their status by producing their distinctive ration books. Other domestically grown fruit such as apples still appeared from time to time, but again the sellers imposed their own restrictions so that customers were often not allowed to buy, for example, more than one apple each. Game meat such as rabbit and pigeon was not rationed but was not always available. Bread was reduced in quality during the war but not formally controlled. An order was passed that bread must not be sold to a customer until the day after it was baked: the stated reasons were to reduce usage because it is difficult to slice just-baked bread thinly; the tastiness of just-baked bread is likely to encourage people to eat it immoderately.

In May 1942 an order was passed that meals served in hotels and restaurants could not cost over 5 shillings (25p) per customer, and could not be of more than three courses, and only one if any of those courses could contain meat or fish or poultry (but not more than one of these). Fish was not rationed but the price increased considerably as the war progressed. The government initially allowed this, since it realised that fishermen would need to be able to collect a premium for their catch if they were risking enemy attack while at sea, but prices were controlled from 1941. However, like other non-rationed items fish was rarely freely available as supplies dropped to 30% of pre-war levels, and long queues built up at fishmongers and at fish and chip shops. The quality of wartime chips was often felt to be below standard, because of the low-quality fat available to fish fryers.

The Bombing of Aveton Gifford

My tuition continued. My mentor Frank Maddever taught me how to stop a bolting horse with a young nervous horse called Royal who would bolt if he heard a sudden noise like a motor bike back firing. I was to hang on to his right ear with my arm over his neck, and press the passageways above his nostrils with the fingers of my left hand thus stopping him breathing and bringing his head down, but endeavouring in the process to keep my feet off the ground so as not to be dragged underneath him or whatever cart or implement he was pulling. There was a genuine anxiety that someone would be hurt by his antics. It was to be for real within six weeks.

On 26 January 1943 I set off at daybreak riding Prince and leading Royal, determined to plough an acre with a single furrow plough: in those days anyone who did this was a man. I had marked out the acre with hazel twigs the day before, and had taken my lunch and nose bags of feed for the horses.

By 3.30 pm I knew I could call myself a man by nightfall. Then behind me to the east I heard a sound of multiple engines. I stopped the horses and went to Royal's head to calm him. Suddenly planes appeared flying low, swooping on the sleepy village below me, its chimneys emitting smoke straight up into the windless clear sky as the women stoked up their stoves in preparation for their returning husband's tea. The searchlight site was in a deep valley 200 yards away and in the next field below I could see the soldiers running in all directions like ants do when you remove a stone over its nest.

Devastation

I saw the dust rise above the church as the first bomb demolished it, and then the Rectory was hit. The horses took off. I was desperately hanging on to Royal and trying to keep his head down, right across my beautiful ploughing, until they reached the bottom hedge and stopped. By then I had counted six Focke-Wulfs hedge-hopping the hills and valleys out over Bigbury Golf Course. Only one had spotted the search light site and turned to attack it; he dropped his bomb 50 yards short which did no real damage whilst machine gunning the search lights. The horses had ended up directly in line with them, and I could hear the bullets striking the bushes to my right. I heard the chatter of the ancient Lewis machine gun, and saw bits flying off the tail of the plane which was no more than 30 feet above my head. I held eye contact with the helmeted German pilot for several seconds until he too passed out of sight. Years later I was to hear he machine-gunned haystacks and corn ricks on his way out over East Allington towards the sea, and frightened the daylights out of Mr Luscombe's eldest son who was harrowing a field. Just beyond Torquay he was shot down into the sea by a Typhoon fighter piloted by a Rhodesian. After my anger had subsided, and reflecting on the death of my brother, that German pilot, and subsequently the Rhodesian a few days later, I was overcome by the futility of human conflict and still am strongly opposed to war.

I galloped those horses home as fast as I could. I was met by my father who assured me he and Mum were alright; he took the horses and sent me into the village to do what I could to help. The devastation was indescribable. Women were appearing covered from head to foot in soot, and their cheeks had rivulets of white down them where they had been crying. I did not recognise them until I heard their voices. Whole roofs were slipping into the street which was covered in slates and nails. I helped open jammed doors, and helped women from out under tables where the ceilings had collapsed trapping them underneath. I headed for the end of the village opposite Wesley Terrace to look for Edi Elliott, our workman Bill's Aunt. By then the emergency services were arriving. I saw Mrs Elson being stretchered out of her house; she had been taking in her washing from the garden when she was hit by a door, breaking her arm and knocking her unconscious. A fire engine passed slowly along on flat tyres, punctured by the nails in the road. By then I was joined by Bill, and we found his Aunt in the garden with her caged budgerigar covered with a cloth "so Joey would not see the devastation of their house". Totally in shock she was calling for her cat. I told Bill to take her home to my mother. I heard that Mrs Payne and some evacuees were trapped in the Rectory and went to help, but rescue workers were already there, so it was back home to help with the milking.

Father by then was in charge of the Rest Centre in the School which was occupied for a couple of weeks by bombed out people until they could be found accommodation. As for our bombed out couple, although we had a perfectly good bath, Edi insisted on using their tin bath (which had miraculously escaped the bombing) in front of the kitchen stove on Saturday nights. My mother was banned from her kitchen while Bill bathed and changed his clothes, a lengthy procedure which lasted for three hours. It was supposed to be for six weeks but it was six months before their home was made fit to live in.

Meeting Sheila for the first time

I mentioned the evacuation of the Battle Training Area and my help in the baling of hay. I remember one day when we were baling in the Slapton Area. I was stacking bales and looking across the valley, and I could see a girl getting cows in to be transported to another farm. I was struck by the grace of her movements; she almost floated over the uneven ground, and in fact I was reprimanded by my boss for allowing the bales to pile up behind the baler. The months went by, D Day and the invasion of Normandy was past the critical stage, and it must have been September because the ram was in with the ewes. I had gathered the flock and was tending to a sheep's feet beside the footpath to the house, when Miss Ilbert brought a new girl in replacement to the girl who had caught cow pox, and as usual Miss Ilbert strode purposefully ahead. It had been raining and the girl hopped over the puddles with such grace that I knew I had seen her across that valley in Slapton seven months before. I straightened up from the upended ewe between my legs to glance again. Just then the ram, jealous of my interference, butted me up the backside sending me catapulting over the ewe into the mud and muck. The girl stifled a laugh and in that lovely lilting voice enquired if I was alright. That was how I met my wife.

Delia, David and Trix in his garden June 2013

Acknowledgements

David Balkwill for writing this unique life story and for his continuing support and answering my endless questions.

Ann and Richard Balkwill, for the loan of family photographs and the family tree.

For the use of photographs and further advice, Holly Trubshawe and staff at The Cookworthy Museum.

Ken Doughty for his wisdom and guidance.

Peter Javes, Jackie Javes, and Ros Brousson for proof reading and continuing support.

Colin Herbert for the loan of photographs.

Neil Cooper for his cover design & expert advice on illustration & photography.

Ged Shelley for his technical drawing skills for the map of Court Barton.

Delia Elliott - December 2013